Pulling Myself Tc

BY

ARTHUR H. HALE

(WITH ILLUSTRATIONS)

BULLFINCH PUBLICATIONS

1986

Also by Arthur H. Haley

THE CRAWLEY AFFAIR
Published by Seeley Service Ltd., (1972).
IN preparation:
OUR DAVY.
The Life and adventures of
General Sir David Baird (1757-1830).

For Barbara
with love and gratitude

Produced by Thomas Loughlin, Mulberry House, Canning Place, Liverpool L1 8JG.

Origination by Bullfinch Publications.

Paperback.
Published by Bullfinch Publications, Hunts Cross Avenue, Woolton, Liverpool 25.

PHOTOGRAPHS & ILLUSTRATIONS.

ACKNOWLEDGMENTS

In 1979 when I began to jot down these childhood memories, the LIVERPOOL DAILY POST kindly inserted my letter asking for information about the old Army Camp at Llanfaes in Anglesey. The response produced a mass of material and renewed acquaintances after more than half a century.

Miss Sallie Williams of Beaumaris gave me the cartoons and photos of the Camp. J W Clarke wrote from Chelmsford and sent me the photo of the mules. Fred Shipperlee gave me valuable information. Brigadier A P Trevor DSO, wrote me letters about the times and gave me contacts. Among them was Kyffin Williams RA, (the little boy I had known at Bryn Hyfryd as as John), and whom he rightly described a 'a mine of information' about people and events in Anglesey. Enid and Geraint Madoc Jones, daughter and son of my old Headmaster at the Grammar School have sent me numerous letters and articles written by Geraint on local subjects. I have visited Katy Matthews, my teacher at Penmon and talked of old times. Others include Emrys Owen and his wife Olwen who was in my class and her brother Iorwerth. I have been back to my old home several times. Now modernised and renamed ARGOED, its owner, Sheila Perry has made me welcome and is keenly interested in its history. My researches on the cartoonist B E Handley led me to Rochdale where John Cole, the head of Local Studies gave me much information and put me in touch with the artist's brother A T Handley, who remembers visiting the Camp as a schoolboy. I have to thank the Gwynedd Archives Service for permission to publish photos of the Bridge at Llangoed and the Cab Stand at Beaumaris: A Giles Jones, Archivist at Bangor University for material and | advice; and O T Rowlands, an old schoolfellow, for the photo of the Class Penmon in 1922. I have also found much information in the files of the NORTH WALES CHRONICLE.

Sadly, Brigadier Trevor, Geraint Madoc Jones and Fred Shipperlee are no longer with us.

INTRODUCTION

My father had a maxim for most occasions. Having had them ground into him in his Victorian childhood, they pointed the way on the map of life he carried in his head.

One of his favourites was: "Pull yourself together."

"For goodness sake boy, pull yourself together," he'd say brusquely if I happened to be distressed over some childish mishap. "It isn't the end of the world. Now is it?"

Put that way I had to admit it wasn't. Not that that was any help at the time. It made me feel worse for not coming up to his standards. And yet, I realise now, those repeated admonitions must have registered. I've been trying all my life with varying success to pull myself together.

I suppose Father must have tried too. But in the end, like all the rest, he had to give up. Nature, as always, had the last word and settled the matter for him with a stroke that left him paralysed from the waist down.

The news reached me by telegram one Friday in late February 1947, from my sister Winnie. Father was seriously ill, it read, and was not expected to last long. I was to come as soon as possible.

It was not entirely unexpected. He was in his 84th year and had already suffered two mild strokes. The third was expected to prove fatal. So as I held the telegram and looked at the words, my feelings were not so much of sorrow but that for me at least this was something more than the passing of an old man. That with his going, the last page would be turned and the book finally closed on the world I'd known as a child.

Next morning I rose early to be off on the road from Liverpool to North Wales. It was bitterly cold for we were in the grip of the seven week frost of that year. The unheated coach, (that I still thought of as a charabanc), meandered along the coast road to Bangor through a countryside white and frozen rock hard from the mountains to the sea.

At Bangor came a stamping wait at the bus stop outside the railway station. Then on to the bus and across the Menai Bridge, twisting along the familiar route that hugged the Straits for most of the seven miles, to be dropped off, half frozen outside the old home in Anglesey.

1

I was met at the door by both my sisters. Winnie looked as impassive as ever, her emotions hidden. Edith, not long arrived from her home in Lincolnshire, as usual, smiling and communicative. They took me into the 'front room' where Father was lying in his bed, taken in there for convenience and kept warm by a roaring fire in the kitchen range. He looked ashy pale and had perceptively withered in the nine months since I had last seen him. He was either asleep or unconscious.

Edith settled down with her knitting to sit beside the bed. She said he might come to at any time and would call me when he did.

In the back room I tried to converse with Winnie as she went about her chores. It was heavy going. We'd been close companions in our early years. But since then we had moved in such widely different spheres we were now worlds apart. She had always been Father's favourite and had taken good care of him in the four years since Mother died. Whether she resented losing those four years I couldn't be sure. I suspected she did. She was 36 and unmarried. The rest of us had taken her for granted for at the time it had seemed her natural role to look after the old man.

I felt grateful but didn't quite know whether to say so. It might do more harm than good by bringing her resentment to the surface. Instead we spoke of Father's going, anticipating the event as people do of the very old. Happy release. Had a good innings. No good prolonging the agony.

I felt relieved when Edith came to the door and said in a half-whisper:

"He's awake. You'd better come now. I think he'll know you."

I went in with her and stood by the bed. Father's eyes had opened with a child-like look of contentment.

"Here's · Arthur come all the way from Liverpool to see you."

Recognition came slowly in a faint smile. Then he said distinctly:

"I havn't done so badly, have I?"

That would have struck me as an odd question at any other time coming from him to me. Now it seemed strangely appropriate.

"You've done fine," I said reassuringly.

He smiled again, satisfied, and looked up at the ceiling. I asked how he was feeling and went on to murmur some trivialities. He seemed not to hear. Thinking he had drifted off again, I was about to leave the room when he chuckled to

2

himself.

"I tricked them," he said.

"When was that?"

"Oh, long before your time. When I first came to Plas Gwyn. I was courting a local girl and the Welsh lads didn't like it. I was a foreigner to them, you see. They were waiting for me in the dark. But the girl told me what they were up to."

He chuckled again.

"I tricked them all right. I went a roundabout way back home and they had a long wait for nothing."

His voice tailed off. I waited till he closed his eyes, then went quietly out of the room.

An hour later I left the cottage that had been home for more than thirty years and set off for my newly found one in Liverpool, knowing that the end would soon come.

On the way I thought of Father's little crow of triumph over the Welsh boys. It seemed so irrelevant at such a time. He hadn't mentioned Mother. I supposed there was no need. They'd celebrated their Golden Wedding six years before. He believed they would soon be reunited.

The remembrance of that Welsh girl must have surfaced at random out of all the events of his long life – millions of tiny incidents and thoughts – happy, sad and humdrum – all interlocked into a gigantic jigsaw that would be completed with his last breath and in the same instant, shattered.

A week later I returned for the funeral. It was still freezing hard. But on the Isle of Anglesey extremes of climate are tempered by the sea. The crust of frozen earth could be broken and the interment was not delayed.

For the first time ever I travelled to the little church at Llanfaes in the luxury of a motor car. The Vicar conducted the ceremony with his usual flat solemnity. At such times he was punctiliously at his best. He did not come in the house before or after. Nor was he expected to. He was a shy man and would have been uneasy.

All the family were there. Ernie at 51 the eldest, Edith, Jack, Winnie and myself. It was the last time we would all be together. Without the magnet of the old home and with Father gone, the last links in the chain were broken. Yet in a part of my mind, the events of the little slot in time we had together, in an age that has long since gone, remain as alive as those of yesterday.

3

1

If living to a ripe old age depends on ones ancestors, then Father's chances would not have been highly rate. Mother used to say he worried about it for some time after they were married. What on earth would she do if anything happened to him? How could she manage the children and see to their future? Above all, what would she do for money.

This was, of course, in the days of 'self help' and the final degradation was 'going on the parish'. Mother begged him not to worry. She'd manage. She had good friends who'd see she didn't starve. She had a pair of hands and if the worst came to the worst she could take in washing.

This did nothing to reassure Father. The idea of Mother having to take in washing only added to his worries.

"Stop talking nonsense, woman," he'd say. "You couldn't possibly make ends meet."

Mother soon gave up trying to reason with him. Given time he'd forget it and be cheerful again. Unless, that is, he thought up some other worry such as the iniquities of the Liberals, green fly on the roses or the machinations of David Jones the butler with whom he had a simmering feud.

His worries were to prove groundless. But on the evidence his chance of approaching the magic three score years and ten must have appeared slim. For three generations the only member of his family on the paternal side to grow old was his great-grandmother, Mary Bramhall, born 1783, in the mining town of Wombwell in Yorkshire who married John Haley, a carpenter

By the Census of 1841 she was a widow living with her son Joseph, also a carpenter at 12 Brown Hill. Aged 29, Joseph was married to another Mary, sister of George Coldwell the blacksmith who lived next door. They had numerous children but by 1851, while Joseph and his mother were still alive, his wife was dead and only George, (my grandfather) and four younger brothers and sisters were left.

In spite of this mortality, Joseph seems determined to give his children a good start in life for he kept them at school until they were 13 or death intervened.

Ten years later no trace is to be found of the family in

4

the Wombwell Census. Joseph and his mother were dead and the children had either died or left the area. George, having served his apprenticeship as a shoemaker, (cordwainer as they were then called), had moved to Southport where he was plying his trade in fashionable Lord Street and was married to Mary Tilston, a young woman of his own age, who had migrated from her native Gresford to take up service with a wealthy family in the Town.

Tilston is not a common name. In the first half of the 19th Century it seems to have been confined mainly to South West Cheshire and the adjoining borders of Flint and Denbigh where they were earning their living as small farmers, farm-labourers, wheelwrights, coachmen, blacksmiths, shoemakers – trades that have now nearly all disappeared.

Mary's father was a gardener and unusual for a Tilston, a Methodist. In 1836 he had to go through the church marriage ceremony with Elizabeth Lewis of nearby Hope as the only legal way of making 'an honest woman of her'. but had none of his children christened in church.

Mary remained a Methodist but probably to please George was also married in church though this had long ceased to be a legal necessity. In 1861 she bore a daughter named Anne and two years later was expecting another when George died. He was 26 and the cause of his death is a mystery as no record exists in Chancery House. Perhaps too overwrought to register it Mary returned to her relations at Gresford where in November 1863 my father was born.

Dependence on others was irksome to Mary but she could not avoid having Father christened in the Parish Church. Not long after she solved the problem of his upbringing by placing him in the care of her Uncle Bill, another gardener, then in his fifties. Bill was a kindly man and in Mary's opinion, too indulgent by half in the way he brought Father up.

Father always spoke of his Uncle with affection and told several anecdotes about him. The only one I remember was about Bill's dog, a terrier of doubtful pedigree, and this I think is because of the mixed feelings it aroused in me.

One winter's evening they were sitting round the hearth. Uncle Bill had dozed off with the dog at his feet. His wife got down on her knees to stoke up the fire and to ease herself up put her hand on her husband's knee. The dog opened an eye and went for her.

Father seemed to think this a fine example of the dog's faithfulness to its master. I felt more concern for his poor

5

aunt and wondered whether she had been badly bitten. But not daring to question Father I kept my feelings to myself.

Mary soon went back into service and a few years later married a gamekeeper named Davies. She saw little of Father though she kept Anne with her and went on to raise a family of three boys, outlived her second husband and was employed as house-keeper in several large houses. At one in Surbiton occurred what she regarded as a highlight in her career.

She had gone to see Queen Victoria at a public celebration when the Queen turned in her coach and smiled directly at her. Convinced of this and regarding it as signal honour it remained a source of great pride in her old age.

Like her father she carried her beliefs and prejudices to extremes. As a Methodist and Liberal she had reservations about Father who had been raised C of E and Conservative by Uncle Bill. She refused to have anything to do with the eldest of her other three sons, a horse-breaker by trade, because she disapproved of his wife.

A photograph taken at the turn of the century 'by Electric light' at the Star Photographic Studios in Oxford Street, reinforces the impression of a woman of spirit and strong will. I wonder how Father would have fared under her influence. He would certainly have been exhorted to pull himself together. And it was probably from her that he inherited the strain that ensured his longevity.

Although the Compulsory Education Act had not yet been passed, Uncle Bill kept him at school until he was 14. He was thoroughly grounded in the Three Rs with the regular threat of a cane 'as thick as my thumb'. The results were an ability to spell that I never remember faulted, a love of reading and an armoury of quotations from folklore, the Bible and the Victorian novelists with Dickens as his particular favourite.

He knew a few poems by heart, including the now almost forgotten EVE OF WATERLOO by Byron. He was fond of reciting the first two verses, dramatically stressing the pauses and sudden changes of mood.

There was a sound of revelry by night,
And Belgian's Capital had gathered then,
Her beauty and chivalry, and bright
The lamps shone o'er fair women and brave men;
A thousand hearts beat happily; and when
Music rose with voluptuous swell,
All went merry as a marriage bell;
But hush! hark! a deep sound strikes like a rising knell:

6

Did ye not hear it? -No; 'twas but the wind,
Or the car rattling o'er the stony street;
On with the dance; let joy be unconfined;
No sleep till dawn, when youth and pleasure meet
To chase the flying hours with flying feet -
But hark - the heavy sound breaks once more,
And nearer, clearer, deadlier than before;
Arm! Arm! It is - it is - the canon's opening roar.

To set the perspective it may be remembered that the time he was learning the poem was nearer to Wellington, Napoleon and Waterloo than we are to World War I. The Great Duke had not long died and there were still Waterloo veterans around telling their tales of the Battle. The Crimean War and the Indian Mutiny were fresh in public memory.

On his leaving school it was only natural for Uncle Bill to apprentice Father in the gardens of a local estate. He made rapid progress in the arts of his profession for at the age of 21 he was appointed head gardener to Miss Ellen Pritchard, then living with her widowed mother at Plas Gwyn, a large mansion near Pentraeth in Anglesey. At near 40 years, Miss Pritchard was known as a daring horse-woman not only after the hare in Anglesey but the fox in Leicestershire.

A stranger in any rural community a hundred years ago was an object of suspicion. For Father the problem was compounded by the language barrier. For although born within the borders of Wales, he arrived in Anglesey unable to speak a word of Welsh and with no trace of an accent.

At work there was no difficulty as the people he was with spoke English. But in an attempt to enter into the life of the community he decided to teach himself Welsh, apparently with the help of a school primer. Welsh is phonetic so having learnt the alphabet he could soon speak the most common words and phrases. His accent was so atrocious as to invite ridicule. Years later I used to wince on the rare occasions I heard him speak it.

Perhaps it was fortunate that most of his time was taken up with the long day's work, for in Summer 12 hours was quite normal. Yet he was a great one for walking with the curiousity and energy to explore the surrounding district in what spare time he had. Roads were still primitive. He used to say they were made by just shovelling stones of different sizes together with clay on the surface and leaving it to be levelled off by horse traffic and pedestrians.

"They wore your boots out in no time. And if you had corns, walking could be agony at times."

7

To increase his mobility he acquired a second hand penny-farthing bicycle. He said mounting it was easy. But there were two ways of dismounting one had to be wary of. One was running over an unusually large stone or getting into the deep rut made by the wheels of farm carts. The other was injudicious use of the 'spoon' brake that operated on top of the solid rubber tyre of the big front wheel. Too much pressure would lever up the small back wheel and project one forward in an arc over the top.

There were other hazards. Dogs, attracted by the bike's unusually rapid progress, went barking and snarling for his heels. Local boys too, who were in the habit of stoning any stranger, were particularly attracted by such a fast-moving target.

His first ride to Beaumaris was hair-raising. Forgetting that Red Hill which runs half a mile into the Town centre, has a gradient of 1 in 7, he had travelled 50 yards before realising the bike was gathering speed at an alarming rate. He applied the brake gently. The back wheel lifted and began to slew round before settling back on to the road.

The steepest gradient is fortunately at the top. But his speed was now such that even on the gentler slope he could only apply the brake in the most tentative manner. The road too was winding, making it impossible to see ahead for any distance.

His fervent hope was to avoid a collision with a cart, carriage, pedestrian or animal in the way. And if the coast by good fortune was clear, that the brake would pull him up before he reached the sea-front.

At the first row of houses a dog on the pavement sighted him and decided to join in the fun. It took up the chase with delighted yelps. Several other mongrels of varying sizes joined in. People turned to look. Some got hastily on to the pavement shouting in alarm to others.

Passing the church the hill steepens again but his speed had slackened enough for him to apply the brake gingerly. To his intense relief he managed to pull up just as he reached Castle Street where a farm cart was trundling across his path.

Needless to say, from then on he used to walk down Red Hill. Some time later, not only the memory of that ride but the large house that took its name from the Hill was to assume a prominent place in his thoughts.

8

2

As Father suffered from the common Victorian tragedy of early mortality, Mother was victim of another. Her father, John Peers Johnson,(Peers was his mother's maiden name and tacking that on was not unusual), was born in Liverpool in 1838. Most of his family were artisans, his father being a turner in wood and ivory while John was a joiner and cabinet maker.

In 1859 he married Esther Banks, daughter of a car driver who hailed from Knowsley on the outskirts of Liverpool. It is noticeable that while John and the best man signed their names, Esther and her bridesmaid only 'made their marks' on the marriage certificate.

The Johnsons moved house several times, probably to be near his work, as cheap public transport was not yet developed. My mother was born in 1873 at Wellington Place, off Mill Street, near the South Liverpool Docks. She was christened Margaret Bentley. I once asked her about the 'Bentley'. She said with evident pride that it was an allusion to a distant, more affluent branch of her family.

She remembered her mother as a long-suffering victim of circumstance; her father as a Jeckell and Hyde. For weeks he would attend to all the wants of the family, taking the children for walks in and around the dock area, patiently explaining all that was going on. In the evenings he would read to them and impart interesting pieces of information he had picked up in his own reading.

Then would come the Saturday night they all dreaded. He would arrive home late and sometimes in a drunken frenzy. Mother, as a small child was hidden inside a cupboard under the stairs where she would crouch, shaking with fear. The drinking would continue into the next week for as long as the money lasted. Its end would be signalled by her father putting his tools into pawn to get the last drinks. Yet he was apparently so good a craftsman that his employer would advance him the money to redeem his tools and start another period of sober industry.

How it all ended is uncertain. I never questioned Mother about the matter when I grew older and by then I think she wanted to draw a veil over her unhappy childhood memories. It seems poor Esther died and the older children left home. The two boys emigrated to Canada and Mother had lost all touch with them. She was herself taken in by an aunt who raised her strictly in accordance with Victorian ethics.

She never saw her father again. His last known appearance was some years later at the house of his daughter Nellie in Gloucester Road Bootle. Seven years older than Mother, Aunt Nellie was married to a master mason and the only aunt I ever got to know. Frail looking and tight lipped, she had a sharp tongue, a will of iron and a caustic sense of humour.

She knew that her father's drunkenness had landed him in prison on at least one occasion. He arrived unexpectedly at the door with a hard luck. story though he insisted he was not begging. To prove it he produced some small picture frames he had made. She gave him a few shillings for the frames and sent him on his way.

I have three of them. Now almost a hundred years old, they are carved with straight chisel cuts and the joints slot together with hair-breadth accuracy.

On leaving school Mother was trained as a children's nannie and at the age of sixteen went to Red Hill, (the large house standing in its own grounds already mentioned), in charge of a family of small girls. In the house were several more girls, daughters of the mistress by a former husband, some being as old as Mother.

This was a happy time in Mother's life and in the two years she was there formed friendships that were to prove lifelong. Between her and the 'Young ladies' the niceties of 'class' were understood and observed. Yet years later when they called to see her one could sense the genuine warmth of affection on both sides.

As a teenager I began to resent the obvious inequalities and injustices of the old class system. Now, while not regretting its virtual disappearance, I can view it with detachment and recognise the stability and happiness it brought to the lives of many. Sometimes I doubt whether the meritocracy that has replaced it has brought much advantage to some at the lower end of the scale.

Mother was a pretty girl, five feet three inches tall, small featured with blue-grey eyes and a mass of light brown hair coiled in a bun after the fashion of the day. Her waist, constrained by corsets, was 18 inches. She had no shortage of suitors. Years later, a rejected one who called in, looked at her and whispered to Edith that he'd never found anyone to touch her.

13

14

She met Father at a ball arranged by the gentry for their servants and the townspeople of Beaumaris. I think it took place at the Town Hall after the Annual Hunt Ball. Dancing went on into the early hours of the morning though it was the rule that all had to be back at work on time next morning. Father used to say that not much work was done that day and this was generally understood and condoned by all except the worst employers.

They were married in Llanfaes Church on 21st December 1891 and set up home in a tiny two roomed house behind the old disused smithy just below the church. Both the smithy and the house are still standing. I have the bill for the furnishings which came to £17 4s 4d.

Mother of course gave up work and settled down to housekeeping and preparation for the arrival of children. In the tiny isolated village it was quiet and at times lonely with Father leaving for work soon after 7 and returning at all hours. Yet after the sordid scenes of Liverpool's dockland, it seemed to Mother a kind of paradise.

People used to call, a few friends, a few curious ones, hawkers and tramps. The Vicar, the Rev J L Kyffin, came regularly. Sometimes he would say:

"I've noticed a shady looking character hanging about. If you'll give me a chair I'll sit outside the door until he moves off."

The shady looking character would have been a hawker or tramp for whom the narrow winding lanes and tall hedgerows gave excellent cover. Like the gypsies, these drop-outs from society were disliked and regarded with suspicion and fear, though their crimes were mostly confined to petty thieving.

Although getting on in years Mr Kyffin was well able to look after himself as a recent incident in Beaumaris showed. A Non-conformist minister had preached a routine sermon in which he roundly condemned the morals and behaviour of the Town's young people. One evening Mr Kyffin was mistaken for the preacher and set upon by two youths when walking down a back street. They found their mistake when he laid one out, picked him up and advised them to be more careful in future.

My parents' first child was born in July 1983, but lived only eight hours. Then in August the following year came a son who was christened George Tilston. The intention was once again to perpetuate the family name. He became known as Tillis to differentiate him from his father.

When a second baby was expected and the smithy cottage being too small for the growing family, a move was made to

15

304, HIGH STREET & CHAPEL STREET,

BANGOR. *Nov 18* 1891

M⟨...⟩ *Haley*

⊰ BOUGHT OF **CHARLES POZZI,** ⊱

LOOKING GLASS AND HARDWARE DEALER.

GLASS AND CHINA WAREHOUSE.   MARINE STORE DEALER.

		Tons	Cwts.	Qrs	Lbs	@			
1	Sett Washing Stand Wardrobe						4	—	
2	Chairs 3/						6	—	
1	Towel Rail						4	—	
1	Sett Fire Irons						3	6	
1	Fender						2	0	
1	Bedstead					2	9	—	
1	Flock mattress					1	8	0	
1	Couch						18	—	
4	Chairs 4/6						14	6	
1	Table 14/6						5	—	
1	Sett Fire Irons 5/						6	6	
1	Jolly tub & body						.	10	
1	Frying Pan						15	—	
1	Chairs 7/6 7/6						1	6	
1	Cast Iron ash Pan						1	11	
1	Iron 5 grtt of Jug 1/6						1	6	
4	Tumblers 3/								
							12	3	3

	Forward	£12.	4	3
1	Feather Bed		2 .. 15	0
1	Clg rug		8	4
1	bucket 10 · 1 shovel 6		1	4
1	dripping tin 6 1 Knife board		1	
1	trivets 6 · 1 tin Can 6		1 .	
1	Candlesticks		8	
2	Flat Irons		2 .	0
1	saucepan 4/6 2/3 1/		7 .	9
1	mat 9/- 1 broom 1/9 1/7		3	9
1/	Knife fork 2		6	
1/	Handle 2			2
1	Hand brush		1	
1	Black lead brush 8 1/		1	
1	scrub brush			
1	shoe brush 1/ 8		6	
1/3	broom 8/		1	8
1	broom 1/		2	6
1	tray 1/9		3	0
1	wash up		1 .	9
			1 .	8
		£17 .	4 ..	4

Number 9 Mona Terrace in Llangoed. Though quite a new house, it was without running water which had to be carried up the short steep hill from the pump on the Common. Each house had a pig-sty at the back but I don't think we ever kept a pig.

Ernie, the next to arrive was born on 29th February, 1896, the last Leap Year of the Century. He was thus denied a 'real' birthday till 1904 when he was eight. Three more were born at Number 9. Edith in 1899, Jack in 1904 and Eira in 1908.

Everyone said what a beautiful baby Eira was. And on the rare occasions that Mother spoke of her it was with a catch of the breath as from some inward pain. For Eira lived only two months. Like the rest she was innoculated for smallpox with the ugly scratches on the upper arm that years later, when changing fashion allowed sleeveless dresses, some girls were inhibited from wearing them. But for Eira it was much worse than disfiguring scratches. She developed vaccine fever and died. Mother blamed the doctor's carelessness and she could well have been right.

The funeral was a sad little affair. Edith, who was eight, did not attend but was sent with Jack across the Common to Mother's friend, Mrs Bloss. From the window she watched the cortege appear slowly down the hill from the Village. Tillis and Ernie were carrying the tiny coffin while Mother and Father with a few friends followed. People on the road side stood in silence as they passed, the men removing their caps and standing with bowed heads. It made its way across the stone bridge over the stream and a few moments later disappeared up the steep hill to the Village church.

No undertaker was involved, only the local joiner for the coffin, the grave-digger and the parson.

Not long after another move was made, this time to the Vicarage cottage at Llanfaes. It's name was Ty Tawel, which means The Quiet House. There in 1910 Winnie was born and in May two years later I, in the phrase then in common use, appeared on the scene.

Ty Tawel was appropriately named. Half a mile from Llangoed, it was far enough in those days to cut off a mother with small children from the life of that community. So for my first five years, for better or worse, I had little contact with other children.

3

The first thing I remember clearly was my fourth birthday in May 1916. I must have been taking in impressions for four years. But they are too confused for recall, like a dream that leaves only a sense of helplessness and vague fears.

This was a happy memory. When I woke that May morning Edith was standing beside my bed. She kissed me on the forehead and said:

"Happy birthday. Look, there's your present."

She was smiling and pointing to a cardboard box on the bed. It was tied with string - to prolong the excitement I suppose. But the knot had a bow, so the untying was easy, I took off the lid and there they were, black, with shining toe caps, shiny brown soles with the stitches showing and at the back of the heels a quarter circle of big square-headed nails. Underneath lay a pair of laces wrapped tightly with glossy red paper and the metal tags showing. Over all hung the unmistakeable tang of newly tanned leather, a scent to trigger instant memory and roll back the years.

I dressed quickly while Edith put the laces in the shoes for me. They were rather big to allow for growing. But with the laces pulled tight they felt as sung as velvet. We walked out into the early sunshine where I stood in my new boots as proud as punch.

Edith was sixteen. Quite old and grown-up to me. When I looked up she seemed amused.

"You're four now, you know."

A sudden thought struck.

"Won't I ever be three again?"

She laughed. "Of course not, silly. You can't go back like that."

"Why not?"

"Oh I don't know. You just can't, that's why. You do ask some funny questions."

I was still puzzled and for some reason felt sorry at not being able to go back to three again.

The philosophical probing was only a momentary digression. Normally I was occupied with worldly matters, worldly in the limited context of our cottage and the grounds it stood in, a plot of about 40 yards by 12.

The cottage was four roomed and square; a fairly large living room, a small kitchen and two bedrooms of equal size. On the north side was a coal-place that held a ton, an earth closet which we called the WC and a shed with the mangle in it. All were of brick except the shed which was brick on three sides but had a corrugated iron roof sloping down to a wooden wall at the back.

From the back door I could look throught the privet hedge that separated us from the Vicarage field. To the left a belt of trees behind a grassy bank hid the gravel drive to the Vicar's 'modest mansion', a hundred yards away. Beyond the field I could see the hills rise gently above the quickthorn hedge to fade into the western sky. On fine summer evenings when the setting sun blazed the sky with reds and gold, Mother would say:

"Just look. There are the gates of Heaven."

She really believed they were. And so did I at the time.

"Always shut the gates after you," the grown-ups kept saying. It still rings in my head like one of those jingling TV adverts. If I forgot and was found out I felt as guilty as if I'd been caught at the jam. One of us or maybe a casual caller would leave ours open and it always seemed to happen on Monday when sheep and cattle were being driven to and from the market at Menai Bridge.

We'd be seated at table when a cow would go loping past the window. Sometimes it would be followed by another. Round they'd come again, stretching out their necks with that stupid, earnest look on their faces that cows have, keeping to the path like a treadmill. I'd watch, fascinated, glad to be safe inside. It was good as a circus and went on till the drover saw what was happening and came on to the path to block their way and shoo them back on the road.

All the water for household use came from the rain on the roof and was collected in wooden casks; two at the back and a reserve one at the front of the house. I used the downspout at the back as a kind of barometer.

"Can't I go out and play now?"

"No, it's still raining."

I'd look out and try again.

"It can't be. The iron's not raining. It's only leaking a bit."

"All right, then. But keep out of the puddles."

The back yard was made up of ashes from the fire and kept in repair by a liberal spread from time to time. The water was supposed to drain down the grid. But the ashes could never produce the smooth, sloping surface for it all to drain off. I found the little puddles could be connected by scratching between them with a stick. The water would flow and the levels would change. Getting wet meant nothing in the thrill of watching the elemental motion that has attracted men's attention down the ages. For a brief moment I was in control of my little world.

"There. Just look at you. How in the world do you get yourself in such a mess?"

Mother reproached but never shouted. Gently but firmly I was propelled inside to be dried out.

Next to a gloomy Sunday, Tuesday was the worst day of the week. Tuesday was wash-day. I hated the damp soapy smell that filled the house on all but the finest days; steamed up the windows that trickled down in little streamlets as soon as I tried to write on them; and if it was raining, all those damp clothes hanging on 'maidens' for hours on end.

Preparations for wash day began on Monday night. Father would fill the kitchen copper with buckets of water from one of the casks. He laid the paper and sticks ready for putting a match to in the morning and brought in a supply of split logs for quick heat that could be controlled by the 'damper'.

For Mother, washing was hard though satisfying work for she had no doubt that cleanliness was next to godliness. She boiled the cottons, using a rod to stir and poke down the parts that billowed up over the steam. For the woollens she had a large galvanized wash-tub and a 'dolly' - like a small three-legged stool with a handle stuck on the top - jabbing and turning till the dirt rose to the top. Then the mysterious blue bag to make the whites whiter than white.

The surplus water wrung out, bare-armed, she would carry the basket full of wet clothes round to the shed where the mangle stood. Occasionally a rat would disappear down a hole in the earthen floor as we went in. That meant a job for Father, putting down pieces of bread and margarine with Rodine spread on and when it had been taken, blocking up the rat hole.

Mangling was hard work as I found later when I grew big enough to do the job. Now Mother had to struggle on her own. First she'd screw down the hand wheel on top to compress the leaf springs and tighten up the rollers. Then she'd fold the garment with a thin edge to ease it in between the rollers with her left hand and with the right grip the handle on the turning wheel. Round the wheel would go, the well greased cogs would slot into each other. Grumbling and groaning the rollers were forced apart and the water began to flood into the bucket set behind to catch it.

When the garment had passed though, the rollers would come together with an almighty thump. Mother gave me the job of seeing that the washing did not fall to the ground at the back. At first I was so fascinated by the working of the mangle that she couldn't really trust me.

"There, you'd have missed that," she'd say as she quickly snatched a woollen vest before it fell.

Out then to the clothes line that ran the length of the garden path on the side nearest to the field. She'd stand on the cinder path pegging up the clothes, glad it was over for another week. For Mother I do believe one of the finest sights in the world was a full clothes line billowing out on a windy day.

In my fifth year I began to realise that I had something wrong with me. I heard my parents talk about it quietly in serious tones. Mother showed a concern that was strangely comforting. The words adenoids and tonsils were mentioned.

The effects were unpleasant yet a part of me. I had no thoughts of how life would be without them. I had cold after cold, a chronic sore throat, deafness of which I was not aware at the time, and if medical books are to be believed, 'a characteristically dull facial appearance', hardly the most endearing qualities in a child.

By my fifth birthday, it was decided something had to be done. The doctor was called in. The adenoids and tonsils had to come out. Arrangements were made for the operation at Bangor Infirmary. But to avoid 'fuss' on my part I suppose, my parents told me nothing about it. All the information I had on this important event in my life came from vague hints and overheard conversation.

One sunny day in June 1917 Mother began dressing herself in her Sunday best and told me to do the same.

"I'm taking you to Bangor to see a doctor," she said. "He's going to cure you of all those colds and sore throats." It would be my first visit to Bangor and it sounded exciting. So on that lovely June afternoon we walked the two miles to Beaumaris, down the pier and on to the waiting steam-boat ferry, the 'Cynfal'. With mingled excitement and consternation I felt the boat shudder and watched the water at the stern as it was churned into a seething foam.

For a few moments we remained level with the pier. Then, quite suddenly we were on our way.

"We'll soon see Bangor," said Mother. "It's just round the bend in the Straits over there at Gallows Point."

I sat fascinated as the pier rapidly receded, getting smaller and smaller in the distance, for that was a sensation I had never before experienced.

The walk from Bangor Pier to the Hospital is uphill and when we got there I felt hot and tired. Mother must have been too for she carried me part of the way, stopping at a sweet shop to buy some chocolate. That was to be a rare treat. The only time I could remember eating chocolate was at Christmas. Mother said it was for me and I should have it later if I was a good boy.

We walked along a verandah and into a room with beds on either side that were empty at the end nearest the door. I stood waiting while Mother talked to a nurse. I saw her pass over the chocolate and heard her say it was for me after the operation. She kissed me and said she would have to leave me now but would be back soon to take me home.

For the first time in my life I was away from home and amongst strangers. The nurse put me in a bed near the door. I lay on my back waiting, my eyes fixed on the open door and the bright sunlight into which Mother had disappeared. I knew there was another older boy in a bed on the other side. But I never once turned to look at him.

Whether I slept or not I don't know. But some time later the nurse was standing beside the bed and with her was a man in white. They talked together. Then the man spoke.

"I'm going to put something over your face and I want you to breathe in deeply."

I saw he was holding a white pad. It came down soft and all enveloping over my nose and mouth and was held there tight. For a moment I struggled to be free. Then the chloroform took effect.

When I came to the nurse was standing over me again. She was speaking in angry tones and handled me roughly, showing me where I had been sick on the pillow. To my misery was added a sense of guilt.

Later another nurse came and tucked me in for the night. Her voice was kind and comforting and I still remember her with overwhelming gratitude.

I must have been in hospital for another two days. From time to time I would cry from weakness, not loud but quietly into the pillow. This annoyed the nurse. She asked me why

I couldn't be like the other boy.

"Look at him," she said. "He's quite happy."

I glanced at him quickly. He was up and playing with a toy. He did not look at me. We were not interested in each other. He was just there and stays in my memory like all that part of the ward as a twilight blur. On the other side the sun still shone and it was there I kept looking to see if Mother would come back.

I had no notion of time. But the other nurse would appear at night and her presence was like a ray of warmth.

By the third day I was feeling better and remembered the chocolate. It loomed suddenly as an important link with home. I asked the nurse if I could have it. She snapped that she knew nothing about any chocolate.

Up to that point I had accepted that everything happening was inevitable and right. Grown-ups knew what was best. Children must do as they were told. Now I knew the nurse was telling a lie. I had seen her take the chocolate. She knew where it was. I dared say nothing. But now I began to hate her.

That afternoon she told me to get dressed as I was going home.

It was Father who came for me, so it must have been a Saturday. I have never been so relieved to see anyone in my whole life.

He carried me piggy back most of the way to the pier. We boarded the Cynfal and sat in the rounded stern. I drank in the warm breeze and watched the green-blue water glide slowly past, hardly saying a word.

Partly from necessity and partly as a treat, Father said we were going to take a ride home. We climbed into one of the horse-drawn cabs waiting in the rank by Beaumaris pier. The coachman flicked his whip and we set off at a steady trot.

I was home. Yet things were not the same. Fears, deep in the recesses of my mind were to haunt me for months to come. Worst were the nightmares. The details have long since receded. But the theme was always the same. I was being smothered.

The dream could come soon after going to sleep. I would come to, desperately fighting for breath, seated on somebody's knee in the light of a summer's evening or in the lamplight before the fire, shaking and bathed in sweat.

Quite suddenly the insane terror would lose its hold as the familiar faces began to materialise - Mother, Father, Edith, Jack - all smiling, anxious.

"It's all right. It was only one of your nightmares. You're all right now."

And it was. Back to the warm bed and a good night's sleep. I had got the fear out of my system - until the next time.

Dr. J.HEPWORTH.

25

4

On winter nights in the War years we used to economise on paraffin by not lighting the lamp till Father came home from work at 6. We sat before the fire in the old-fashioned kitchen range that catered for all our needs in heating and cooking.

Burning both coal and logs the top bars of the front could be dropped forward to hold a pan or kettle. In the oven on the right, Mother did all the roasting and baking, including bread. A hot-plate on the left was large enough to take a couple of pans and when the damper under the oven was fully open the fire roared like a furnace.

Our eyes would sparkle in the glow as the logs crackled and blazed in kaleidoscopic changes of yellow, orange and red to light up parts of the room and cast flickering shadows in the corners. No wonder 'Pictures in the Fire' came up as a regular subject for school essays. Unlike watching TV, gazing into the fire with its rare warmth, set the imagination free to roam unfettered by 'expert' opinion.

Mother used to tell Winnie and me stories. Some were fairy tales but the ones we liked best were about the family. She told us about her own childhood. It seemed so long ago and so different from ours that it too was like a fairy tale. Her life in Liverpool. Her father in all his moods; her poor mother. About drunken women fighting in the streets. Drink, she believed, was the greatest cause of misery and wickedness in the world. She adjured us never to 'let the demon drink pass our lips'.

She told us of 'Her Benny', the story of two Liverpool waifs. Set in the 1890s, it was several years after her own childhood. Ten year old Benny and his younger sister Annie are driven on to the streets each day by their drunken father and step-mother to earn their own keep. Annie has to stand barefoot at a street corner selling matches while Benny offers to carry the bags of gentlemen.

At last, unable to stand their father's cruelty any longer they run away and are befriended by a night-watchman who finds them a place to sleep. Before long Annie dies and after much injustice and hardship, Benny goes on to attain material success.

26

The author, Silas K Hocking, a Methodist Minister, having spent three years in the City, had a genuine sympathy for his characters which he says are drawn from life. Though the story now appears sentimental, and has a strong religious message, it is told with dramatic skill.

It is not going too far to say that Mother identified with the wretched children. She did not have to go barefoot as they did and was never without a home. But memories of her own childhood made it easy to imagine herself in their situation.

I loved to hear about Tillis and Ernie when they were boys. At first I could not remember what they looked like as both were away. Tillis was in the army and Ernie working on munitions in London. This is how they appeared to me later.

Physically and mentally they were complete contrasts. Both were 5ft 11inches tall. But whereas Tillis was slightly built Ernie had broad shoulders and powerful arms, his body tapering towards the feet so that although upright he walked with a slight roll.

Both were sensitive in their ways and this was revealed in their faces. Tillis looked serious and reserved. Yet he had great consideration for others and formed firm friendships. Ernie's eyes were bold and unwavering and I have never known anyone quicker to sense a slight, whether intended or not. He was a good raconteur and rarely content to play second fiddle in company. His friendships could last for months or even years. But the break would come over some trivial misunderstanding and the break would be final.

Intellectually there was little to choose between them; though I believe Ernie was by far the most gifted. Yet Tillis went on to academic success while Ernie finished his formal education at 13. He said in later life this was because he did not want Mother and Father to be burdened with two of them at the Grammar School.

Mother denied this. They were quite willing to send him. But he was determined to earn his living with his hands. I believe she was right. Ernie was rationalising for he felt keenly his lack of formal education without actually saying so.

As boys they used to fight. Over what I never found out. Their differing attitudes to life at that early stage was probably the cause. When Tillis was 12 and Ernie 10, matters came to a head. They had a fight that turned deadly serious and Tillis was badly beaten. Ernie had established his physical **superiority** and they never fought again. Soon after they

27

began to move on different planes.

Tillis went on to the Grammar School at Beaumaris. He did not win a scholarship, but the Vicar, Rev J D Jones, persuaded my parents to give him the chance and they agreed to find the money to pay for him. After a year they were relieved of this burden when he won a special scholarship.

Meanwhile the headmistress had found Ernie impossible to manage. With Murdoch Macdonald, one of several sons of the coachman to Colonel Hampton Lewis, (one of the last survivors of the Charge of the Heavy Brigade at Balaclava), he was transferred to Beaumaris Elementary School and the firmer control of a headmaster.

The Macdonald boys were a lively lot and typified the resentment felt by some of the rising generation at the subservience of their parents to the gentry who exercised such control of their lives. My parents were once acutely embarrassed when Murdoch turned up one evening after dark with a dead pheasant, for unknown to his father, the boys had been poaching on the estate. They salved their conscience by convincing themselves that wasting good food was sinful, plucked the bird, burnt the feathers and made a hearty meal of it.

All but one of the Macdonald brothers eventually emigrated to Canada. Murdoch came back and visited us several times. He told us with evident satisfaction about the pheasant. He and his brothers had gone out the night before the Colonel was to have a shoot and very unsportingly bagged most of the birds when they were asleep. The following day they climbed a tree to watch the Colonel's party and chortled with delight as they saw their annoyance and frustration at the absence of targets.

Of the mischief Ernie got up to I found one piece of firm evidence and one of hearsay. A roof beam in the old school, about 15 feet high, bore his initials, E R H neatly carved on it. How he managed to get up there I have no idea.

The hearsay bit went like this. One Sunday evening during a summer drought, prayers for rain were said in the Church Room. Just before the end of the service, Ernie slipped out and climbed up the oak tree whose branches spread over the entrance. As the congregation solemnly filed out he proceded to pee over them. Dispersed by the dense foliage the drops descended like rain. It seemed for a moment their prayers had been answered.

At 14 he left school and started work as a telegraph boy in Llangoed. Waiting for the telegrams gave him the chance to indulge in the showmanship to which he was inclined He learnt to stand still on his cumbersome bike with outstretched arms, to weave his way slowly zigzag between a row of stones striking each in turn with a rod used as a polo stick.

His most spectactular exploit was to ride slowly along the stone wall of the hump-backed bridge over the stream that runs through the common. The wall, still there, is about 16 inches wide and very uneven. It must have taken a bit of nerve.

The part of the job he disliked most was having to deliver telegrams to Llanddona, a barren, isolated spot in those days. The boys of the village resented all strangers and used to stone him on his way in and out. In his fifteenth year he contracted some illness and lay in bed with a raging fever. From his deranged muttering, the thing that played most on his mind was that he had to deliver a telegram to Llanddona. The fever mounted and it was feared he would lose his life. Dr Hepworth told Mother that he could do no more. The climax would come at mid-night. If he passed that hour he would recover - otherwise - -.

He survived and was apparently none the worse for what had ailed him.

A year later, perhaps from his experience of the telegraph system, he took it into his head to join the Royal Navy as a signaller. The venture proved short lived. Anyone less fitted for the strict routine of the Senior Service than Ernie could hardly be imagined. After a month he got himself discharged by feigning deafness.

He did not return home but went to stay with Aunt Nellie in Bootle where Uncle Matt, the stone-mason, got him a job labouring on the docks. He stood this for a while then friction developed between him and his Aunt whose home was always like a new pin. He would come home dirty and have to wash and change his clothes, whereas Auntie's eldest son Harry, was a clerk who came home as clean as he went out.

So the old controversy of hands versus brains raised its head again. In all this, according to Ernie's account, Uncle Matt was piggy in the middle. At work 'he was a roaring lion'. But as soon as he set foot in the house he became 'as meek as a lamb' and did as he was told. This puzzled Ernie who could never adapt quietly to circumstances.

At last he decided to leave. Without telling anyone where he was going he put his savings on a one-way ticket to London where he arrived at mid-night. He slept on a doorstep and went early to look for a job. He secured one as a blacksmith's striker, which certainly fitted in with his desire to work with his hands.

During his years in London he developed some unsuspected talents. As a boy he could play a lively tune on the tin whistle. Now he acquired a violin and taught himself to play. I still remember his renderings of popular songs like 'Roses of Picardy' and light classics such as well loved melodies from Cavaliera Rusticana and The Tales of Hoffman. He did a lot of sketching and although untaught his draughtsmanship was very fine. Reacting against his upbringing he turned to Socialism and Athiesm, speaking at political meetings and attending gatherings of Freethinkers at the Conway Hall. He became steeped in the writings of Bradlaugh, Joseph McCabe, Voltaire and the like.

It was 1916 when I first remember seeing Ernie. He had been away over four years and there was great excitement at the return of the prodigal. His train was due in Bangor at 5pm so he was expected about 7. But it was always give or take an hour or so depending on the train being on time, catching the ferry to the Garth to save the long trek round by the Menai Bridge and whether one was lucky enough to cadge a lift on some horse drawn vehicle.

The hour passed but he did not come. By 8.30 it seemed there must have been a mishap and Mother was beginning to worry. Then in he walked, all smiles with a big parcel on his back and a small case in his hand.

The train had been late. He'd walked down to Bangor pier and arrived just in time to see the last ferry leave. Nothing for it then but to walk all the way - uphill to the coast road, across the Bridge and along the winding road to Beaumaris; down to Friars Beach and the last uphill climb home. And all after half a day's work and the train journey.

The parcel on his back? Well, in a letter he'd promised Winnie a doll's pram. This was it. To show how fit he was he did a hand-stand on the edge of the kitchen table. His money dropped out of his pockets and Winnie and I yelled and scrambled after it. He'd not brought me a present so he let me keep a half-crown.

I had to hand it over to Mother to look after. But first he made it disappear out of his hand and brought it out of my hair. Conjuring was another of his accomplishments.

My sister Edith left school in 1913. Like all the pupils at Penmon C of E she must have been held back by the poor quality of the education there. But for girls, education was not then regarded as of prime importance. Her first job was

in service in a household somewhere in Shropshire. It was an experience she never forgot.

The place was run by a housekeeper, an aging spinster, who seems to have been mentally unbalanced. Instead of instructing Edith in her duties she expected her to know them. And when they were not carried out to her satisfaction she would resort to invective and throwing things such as plates. After having laid the table for the family, Edith would be called up a long flight of stairs to move a knife or fork a fraction of an inch.

On a rare week-end off Edith came home. Mother was sympathetic. But from Father she received little consolation.

She recalled being in tears as he walked her to Beaumaris to catch the ferry and how the burden of what he had to say went:

"Come on now. This won't do. These things have to be borne. You'll just have to make the effort and pull yourself together."

As she said, "It was always – 'Pull yourself together'. But how could you? There were times when it wasn't possible."

Eventually the stairs brought her release. All the unnecessary climbing brought on leg trouble that on doctor's orders made it essential for her to lay up for a few weeks. She was given the sack and returned home with heart-felt relief.

When she recovered Edith was apprenticed to a woman in Beaumaris who took in sewing for a living. In her two years of apprenticeship she received no pay and was taught little of the finer points of needlework.

She was thus engaged when I became old enough to know she existed. At this time I received more attention from her than anyone else in the family and only wish I had told her so in later life.

5

For my first fifteen years or so religion played an important part in my life.

In my earliest memories I kneeled at my bedside night and
morning to say the Lord's Prayer. In the War years Father
always said grace before meals. though soon after he began
to confine it to the main meal only. In the end he said it
only before Sunday and Christmas dinners to let God know He
was not entirely forgotten.

I had regularly heard the awesome names of God, Jesus
Christ, the Angels, the Devil, Satan, Heaven and Hell and had
formed hazy conceptions of what they were supposed to
mean. They were a joyless and frightening part of life.

When I was four the time had come to attend Sunday
School. The idea was not unattractive. It was held in a large
grey-painted corrugated-iron building which I knew quite well
as it stood only a few yards beyond the fence of our vegeta-
ble garden and less than 50 yards up the road.

As occupier of the Vicarage Cottage, (rent 5 shillings a
week), it was part of Father's unwritten contract to keep
the Church Room in order. This included brushing the floor,
arranging the furniture, tending oil lamps - suspended from
the roof beams and hung on wall brackets - and stoking up
the coke stove in winter.

I'd accompanied him several times and was acquainted with
the lay-out. Entry was through a porch for coats and hats,
leading into the main room where chairs with red hassocks
were arranged in rows on either side of a central aisle. At
the far end on a low stage stood a large table covered by a
white cloth with an embroidered motto in Latin. A lectern
for the preacher stood on its left and on its right a piano,
intended for use at concerts and other secular functions,
though from my recollections these were rare.

Leading up to the stage were three steps to the right of
the vestry door. Two yards from the door the harmonium was
placed sideways on to the congregation. Both sides of the
room had sash windows with frosted glass below for privacy
and clear glass above through which the sky could be seen.

Brightly coloured pictures lined the walls. Some depicted

Christ with long fair hair and a halo as The Good Shepherd, holding a crook and followed by sheep looking up at him with meekly adoring expressions; preaching the Sermon on the Mount or Feeding the Five Thousand. John the Baptist was there too, calling out in the Wilderness. He had black hair.

There were a few illustrations from the Old Testament; David picking up pebbles from the stream while Goliath stood menacingly in the distance; Noah looking pensively from a window in his Ark at a white bird; Samson about to pull down the pillars of the Philistine temple on his enemies.

On the initiation day I was dressed in a sailor suit that had been passed down to each of my three brothers over the past eighteen years. I sat expectantly in a class of a dozen young children, most of whom I had never seen before. There followed an interminable silence broken only by the muted talk of adults, the arrival of late-comers and the whispered cautions to fidgits.

At last the vestry door opened and a figure in white appeared clutching a book in an upturned hand. It stopped just in front of us at the foot of the steps to the stage and began to speak in a strange monotonous voice.
Then: "Our Father which art in Heaven - - -."

I recognised that and joined in with the rest . Of what followed I remember little except the amazing volume of sound from the harmonium, only about two yards away, and that I was trying hard to make sense of it all. What seemed hours later it was all over and I filed out with the rest feeling mightily relieved.

When we got home I joyously announced to Mother that I saw Jesus Christ.

There was a puzzled silence.

"What did he look like?" someone asked.

"He was dressed in white and had a book in his hand."

Edith burst out laughing.

"That was Mr Evans. He's only the Vicar."

I'd meant to say God was there too because I heard someone being addressed by that name. But I was put off by the laughing and lost my nerve. Not long after I found it wasn't God, only an older boy named 'Gordon', one of the Macdonalds in fact. I felt glad then I hadn't mentioned it and been laughed at again.

At five I began to attend the Sunday morning Service in the Parish Church. All the family went except Mother who stayed behind to cook the Sunday roast.

At first I was puzzled about this arrangement. She seemed to be breaking the Commandment to 'Keep holy the Sabbath Day'. When I voiced my misgivings she explained that cooking dinner did not really fall within the Commandment. Some work, she said, was essential, like feeding animals – and people.

I accepted this all the more readily because Sunday dinner was such an oasis in the desert of Sunday austerity. It was easily the best meal of the week; roast meat, roast potatoes, greens in season and rich gravy. Even the creamy rice pudding was special, not to mention fruit from the garden.

Only sickness prevented our going to church. Wind, rain or even snow, we sallied forth and, if necessary, sat through the service in wet clothes. The monotony of the routine was varied only by the weather. If it was wet we walked the narrow winding lane flanked by tall hedges; if it was dry we took the shorter route across the fields.

Either way there were hazards. The lane as far as the Army Camp was easy going though very narrow – just wide enough for a single cart or carriage to pass if we stood against the hedge. But after the Camp the hill was steeper with the surface rutted by farm carts to make muddy rivulets, inches deep when it rained. A false step and you were up to the ankles in water. Fortunately we all wore boots. Men and boys had lace-ups, the girls' were buttoned and required the use of a button hook to fasten them.

At the top of the hill the tall hedge line on the left was broken by a five barred iron gate and there on a fine morning we would pause for a breather to savour the breath-taking grandeur of the scene. Below us, at the bottom of the steeply sloping field, nestled the grey stone church with its taper spire. Beyond stretched the fields and tall trees super-imposed on the level Straits. Then beyond the Straits, rising abruptly, the Snowdon Range.

"You'll have to go a long way to find a better view than that," Father would say. His travels not having extended much further than the borders of Wales, he could hardly have been a great authority. Yet even now, having travelled in four Continents, I don't think he was too far out.

Punctuality was a part of religion, so there was rarely need to hurry down the last very steep 200 yards; the bell would still be tolling when we entered through the North porch into the church.

The fine weather route followed a public footpath along

the edges of the fields. But to reach it we had to cut diagonally across the home paddock where two great black cart-horses and a flock of sheep grazed.

In Biblical and other stories, sheep are depicted as the most timid and helpless of animals. One summer I found there are exceptions. A lamb whose mother had died was raised on the bottle by the farm bailiff who lived in one of the cottages known as Tyn Lon near the paddock. It grew up an object of attention for everyone who entered the field, responding to pats and scratching of the head by frisking round in a playful manner.

It soon grew into a fine sheep, retaining its affinity to humans. Knowing no fear, its playfulness started to take on a less endearing turn. As soon as it saw anyone enter the field it detached itself from the flock, lowered its head and charged like a ram. For so stupid a creature its timing was impeccable. It could stop in full career a mere foot from one's knee. Its playfulness proved its downfall. Because of the consternation roused in the footpath users the wretched victim of human kindness was prematurely despatched to the butcher.

In contrast, Drummer and Jessie, the cart-horses, were pictures of domesticity as they enjoyed their day of rest, cropping the grass, nuzzling each other and lazily flicking off flies with their long tails. In the top corner of the paddock we passed through the first of the kissing gates, beside the stone built stables that sheltered the horses at night and where their harness was hung ready for use on Monday.

On now beside a grassy bank with a low hedge on top that was such a feature of our part of the world. Then over a wooden stile to skirt the edge of another field. And here between the path and the bank was a ditch that drained into a small reedy pond where moorhens nested and where I used to slide on the ice. In Springtime I would jump the ditch to pick a big bunch of the yellow primroses that lay like a carpet over the bank and take them home to Mother.

A right hand turn and along to another kissing gate. Then we would always pause. For in the next and last field the Bryn Hyfryd herd of cattle often grazed with their attendant bull. He was a large, grey, formidable looking fellow with a ring in his nose.

"If he's among the cows there's nothing to worry about," Father said. "But if he's out on his own just keep your eye on him."

How reliable his advice was I am unable to say; I used to keep an eye on that bull wherever he was. I always felt happier when we had rounded the church-yard wall without attracting his attention and passed through the last kissing gate.

As Father was the sidesman taking round the plate, we always sat in the pew nearest the door. Scattered about in the nave in front of us were the rest of 'our class', mainly servants of the local gentry who, by that curious instinct of mankind, always contrived to sit in the same pew. Should a stranger unwittingly invade their territory they would look pained and whisper in annoyance as they plumped themselves down elsewhere.

The gentry had their private pews in the South aisle and entered the church by a side door. The distinction seemed only right and proper - the rich man in his castle, etc. I have since read that the north side of the church was believed to face the domains of the Devil. Was the thought in the minds of the founders of our church as they would naturally see to it that the people of quality were given whatever spiritual benefit could be gained from the belief?

Curiously, therefore, a smaller north aisle, raised to command a view of all the church was taken up by the richly upholstered, inward facing pews of the Williams-Buckeley family. I can recall their putting in an appearance on only one occasion and that so unexpected and dramatic as to rouse a deal of vulgar attention.

Throughout the service my eyes were magnetically drawn to an elderly lady in a splendidly large hat, whose hair seemed to have a blue tinge and whose face was evidently 'painted'. I went home bursting with curiousity. Mother explained that 'painting' the face was quite in order for ladies. But for ordinary women it was extremely vulgar. While accepting this explanation as part of the Devine Order, I was not entirely satisfied. There was a flaw in the logic somewhere though I couldn't put my finger on it.

Apart from this memorable occasion the uniform monotony of the service was rarely broken. The bell stopped tolling. There followed a moment's hush as I waited for the next move. This was the appearance of the verger after his duties of bell ringing. A small man in a dark suit he emerged from the vestry and with head bowed and held slightly to one side walked briskly down the nave, his rubber heels emphasizing the 'clop, clop' as the soles met the stone floor.

He disappeared into the organ loft. A pause as he pumped at bellows. The voluntary blared forth. The white surpliced Vicar emerged from the vestry and the service was under way.

For a small child the hour that followed was a test of endurance. The Vicar's reading of the service was formal and uninspired. Nothing in his sermons could possibly have raised a heart or an eyebrow in the congregation. The curates were little better. Occasionally we had a visiting preacher who would cast a different light on some scriptural text. I still remember one, though of what he said nothing now remains; only that he was cheerful and actually seemed to be happy.

So generally I hated the whole business of Sunday morning and would have done anything to have got out of going. And yet there may have been something in what the grown-ups never tired of saying - "You don't know what's good for you."

I was confined within stone walls. But as the poet said, they 'do not a prison make'. Through the twenty minute sermon I had to sit still. But imagination was free. The dull monotonous droning of the preacher could be ignored. And as for the rest; well, most of it was above my head. But to have been subjected to the prose and poetry of the Prayer Book and the King James Bible, to have it poured over one's passive mind, week after week; how was I to know then that I was receiving a gift beyond price.

Once only was the pious monotony broken. The church was broken into and the poor-box stolen. The box was found in the churchyard, smashed open, its contents gone.

Shocked at the deed yet full of excitement, I set off quite eagerly for once to the service. As I entered the pew there plain to see were the tell-tale broken fittings on the wall from which the box had been wrenched. Above was evidence of how the thief had got in. Where had been a small stained glass window was a rough structure of boards to keep out the draught and any other intruder.

The general opinion was the thief was a tramp. Throughout the service I kept glancing at the boarded up window imagining how he must have come in and half expecting him to reappear. I felt puzzled too as to how he could have brought himself to have done such a dreadful deed. At night too - when ghosts would have been at large. Why was he not struck down dead in the act? He was robbing the poor. Yet he was poor himself. Perhaps he was starving.

The grown-ups dismissed that suggestion. Anyone who did such a thing had only one reason. He wanted the money for drink, they said.

The thief was never caught. The poor-box was repaired and fitted on to the wall again more securely. But in place of the stained glass window, for reasons of economy, a sheet of frosted glass was put in its place.

I felt sad about that. It looked so mean and shabby compared with the bright reds and blues and yellows of the men, women, children and angels with their haloes.

Our Sunday evening services were held in the Church Room. Very different from the one in the morning, it could be called the Working Man's service.

There was the severely functional building of grey-painted corrugated iron with the plain glass windows. In winter it was cold and in summer stifling hot. No parsons officiated and no gentry attended. It never occurred to me to ask why. Perhaps the clergy were worn out by their morning labours. Perhaps the gentry agreed with Lord Melbourne that 'once is orthodox, twice is puritanical'. Whatever the reasons the congregation were happy to have the show to themselves.

The lay preachers who officiated were a mixed bag. They included the Classics Master from the Grammar School, a bank cashier and theological students from Bangor, all practising their skills at preaching.

The schoolmaster was in his thirties, tall, well built and with a nicely domed bald head. As a preacher he lacked inspiration, (just as I found later he did as a teacher of Latin). In his sermons he would invariably make the transition from Christianity to Greek or Latin mythology. Having made it he was in his element and the myths took over to be explained in some detail.

The effect on his congregation was not surprisingly one of mystification and brought from Mother mild protests when she arrived home. She wanted only the most orthodox exposition of the Scriptures served up and suspected there must be some impiety. "I don't see what all those Greek fairy tales have to do with Christianity."

Before very long the master, either from not being asked or from an acceptance of defeat, stopped coming. In fact I wonder why he ever started. Perhaps because he was a man of moods. In school he could be quite jovial at times. At others he would put on a strong, silent man act as when his hat was once knocked off his head by a snowball as he entered the school yard.

He stood waiting until the boy who threw the snowball came up and apologised. He kept looking at the culprit while all activity in the yard ceased. Receiving no further response he said:

"Well. Aren't you going to pick it up?"

The boy picked up the hat, dusted off the snow and gave it to him. He placed it on his bald head, said "Thank you," sardonically and plodded in dignified silence into the school.

His attempts to teach us Latin were not very successful. It was compulsory for the first three years when most of us dropped it with relief. Only one or two went on to take it in School Certificate. Sometimes he became as frustrated as we did as when he grabbed a boy who was fooling about and flung him across the room.

Red in the face he rasped out: "You all saw that. From now on any boy who goes out of line will feel the weight of this left hand of mine."

The threat was counter productive. It became a standing joke to warn each other about that 'powerful left'.

Not long after we observed he was being ostracised by the senior mistress who, like all the women teachers was a spinster. Searching enquiry revealed that she had walked into the mistresses staff room and surprised him kissing a young mistress. We thought him a bit old at 40 for this sort of thing but allowed him a grudging admiration as the mistress involved was the pick of the bunch.

Many years later I met him and we had several long conversations. I was surprised to find him friendly and with a keen sense of humour. I suppose, like many another he had become a schoolmaster, realised his mistake but decided he'd have to make the best of it.

Without saying anything memorable the divinity students were more lively. After the service they would come to our house for tea and cake before walking or cycling back to Bangor. I enjoyed these brief calls. Though never drawn into the talk or venturing a comment, I was surprised to hear them speak jocularly on everyday matters; quite different I imagined from the sombre parsons the would become.

They were always dressed in black and in winter wore black overcoats, very like the one Father had for Sunday best and special occasions. One Saturday afternoon as he was preparing to go on his regular jaunt to Beaumaris he noticed a strange handkerchief and some small change in his coat pockets. "That's funny," he said, "Where on earth did they come from?"

No one knew and a mystery it remained until the Sunday night a month later when the student arrived for his stint. He was wearing his black coat, a replica of Father's and of course it emerged they had picked up each others.

41

"I couldn't make it out," the young fellow said, adding with a slight smirk, "All the way to Bangor I was thinking of a subject for my next visit. I kept my hands in my pockets and there were some bits in one that became quite soft with the warmth. So I kept moulding them into different shapes. It wasn't till I arrived at the digs I found they were bits of candle. Then I put two and two together and realised it must be your coat and you'd popped them in when you were getting the church ready."

Another student set off on his bike, his aceteline lamp burning and with Father seeing him off at the gate. Father had turned to come in when he heard an almighty crash. He rushed back into the road in time to make out the dim figure of the student emerging from the ditch on the far side of the road.

The poor chap, making for the left of the road had turned to wave, gone over too far, caught his front wheel in one of the gulleys in the narrow grass verge that drained the water from the road and gone over the top into the three foot ditch.

He limped back into the house, muddy, wet and bleeding at the knee with sundry other cuts and bruises. He was patched and cleaned up but rejected offers to be put up for the night, saying he had to get back as no one would know where he was. It seems remarkable now that no one suggested contacting the Vicar who was only a hundred yards away.

The only part of the service to give me pleasure was the hymn singing; far better than in the morning. The harmonium bellowed out, the closely knit congregation sang with gusto making the sound reverberate within the confines of the iron-clad room.

Looking through the hymns in the Prayer Book for the first time in years, I find the ones we sang were confined to less than 100 of the most popular of the time. I can recall exactly the effect some used to have on me and the pictures they conjured up of the world as I was beginning to see it.

Onward Christian soldiers

Marching as to war - -

There they were, the khaki clad men from the nearby camp, marching past on their way to France.

I felt bewildered by the contrast in some of the hymns. I could no more reconcile their vindictiveness with 'A Loving God' and 'Gentle Jesus' than I could the week-days' attitudes of people with their Sunday piety.

'When God of old came down from Heaven,

In power and wrath he came - -"

From that I had the vision of the head and shoulders of an angry old man with long grey flowing hair appearing from the clouds.

But I liked some for their romantic imagery:
"From Greenland's icy mountains, From India's coral strand, Where Afric's sunny fountains Roll down their golden sand, From many an ancient river, From many a palmy plain They call us to deliver Their land from error's chain."

There was comfort in: "The day thou gavest Lord is ended. The darkness falls at thy behest."
And in: "God moves in a mysterious way His wonders to perform; He plants his footsteps in the sea And rides upon the storm."

Like all children (perhaps they still do) I loved the rousing "All things bright and beautiful, All creatures great and small - -" Even "The rich man in his castle. The poor man at his gate, God made them high or lowly And ordered their estate," seemed to fit in with life as I first knew it.

"Plough the fields and scatter The good seed on the land," suited the time perfectly. For in season men still walked behind the horse-drawn plough and some could even be seen scattering the seed corn by hand.

The hymn lines that had the most emotive effect on me were: "Happy birds that sing and fly Round thine altar O Most High."
Birds symbolised all the happiness and freedom I longed for as I stood among the sombre people in the grey church on a bright sunny evening. If only I could fly away like the birds. No constraints or Sunday gloom for them. For a few moments I wallowed in wistful misery. Tears well up in my eyes.

6

We all attended the little Church School at Penmon though not all started at the same age. In those less bureaucratic times the starting age seems to have depended partly on the vacancies in the infant class and partly on the wishes of the parents.

Edith began when she was 3, and Jack was 4. That was when they lived in Llangoed and the school was only a mile away. The move to Ty Tawel had given us the choice of two other schools about the same distance away, Beaumaris and Llangoed. They were State Schools, larger that the one at Penmon and the tuition may have been better. But being C/E and occupants of the Vicarage Cottage, there could be no question of changing. Having to walk two miles, however, Winnie and I were 5 when our formal education began.

First day at school is an ordeal for most children. Though I wonder if all the concern that has been voiced and all the research and debate on it have not added to the problem for the sensitive child. We often forget the vague fears roused in young children listening to their parents, to radio and TV.

My difficulties stemmed from two sources; my almost complete lack of contact with other children up to that stage and the divergence of the English atmosphere at home and the predominantly Welsh one in school.

In one respect I was fortunate or not according to one's viewpoint. Nearly all teaching was then in English as no official instruction had yet been issued to compel the use of Welsh. On this very controversial issue I can only speak from experience. It was difficult enough for me just to fit in. To have had to contend with a 'foreign' language would certainly have compounded the problem.

Most of the children were Welsh but were bilingual and there was no animosity against the English minority. The only time this would surface was if I fell out with friends who would exclude me by talking to each other in their native language while the tiff lasted. It was a painful rebuff.

I did try to learn Welsh, but my efforts were greeted with such amusement that I gave up. I got to understand much of what was said and adopted a Welsh accent which has stayed with me over the years; and by a curious reversal, has been known to rouse a degree of racial prejudice - probably due to the stupid 'Taffy was a Welshman,' myth.

On 10th September 1917, fortified with the usual breakfast of porridge ladled out of the double container in which it was cooked and each carrying a small parcel of jam sandwiches for the mid-day meal, Winnie and I set off on the two mile trek to school.

I was used to walking but had never covered the route before. So when we arrived at the school steps I felt a little tired and bewildered. The yard I was taken into first was full of girls - more girls than I'd ever seen before. Some pressed around curiously asking questions and escorting me to the part of the yard allocated to the infants. This was set in an angle of the building between the boys' and girls' yards.

Almost immediately some big boys came round the corner and taking me by the hand, led me away. They talked to me in English but amongst themselves in Welsh. They seemed friendly so I was not alarmed. We came to an enclosure the like of which I had never seen before but soon learnt was the boys' toilets. It consisted of two earth closets and a urinal.

They asked me to take out my 'private parts' which were inspected and from the remarks, I was glad to find, appeared to be to their satisfaction. I was then taken back to the playground amid some good-natured banter that I could not understand but sounded reassuring.

The origins of this initiation I never discovered. It continued for all newcomers over the next two years and then came to an abrupt end, for a reason which will become apparent -as did another custom.

The primitive toilets were separated from those used by the girls by a wall about seven feet high. As I discovered later some of the older boys would sometimes call out ribald remarks that brought reproofs and giggles from the girls' side. But the strongest response was produced by a quite small boy who earned for himself respect and admiration for a feat he could perform on request. This was to direct a jet of pee, in way I leave to the imagination, over the seven foot wall on to the girls' side, thus provoking squeals of outraged protest.

My first day in the class room proved a disappointment.

There were more than a dozen infants with a young man in charge. Who he was and how he came to be teaching infants I have no recollection. But I do remember he had little control over them and didn't seem to care. He was amused at one fat little boy who kept running over the desk tops. He laughed and smacked the boy gently on the bottom, to everyone's amusement.

He made a perfunctory attempt to make us work. For reading we had some well-thumbed cloth-bound books that began with the usual pictures of an apple, a ball, a cat - with the first letter in large print, capitals and small, and the name spelt out underneath. For writing we had slates to copy from the blackboard. The only apparatus in the room was some frames with large beads on wires for counting. I longed to have a go at these but was not given the chance. In fact I cannot recall their ever being used.

In the afternoon I enjoyed a brief spell of glory. The teacher asked if anyone could tell a story. I raised my hand and said I knew on called 'The tale of Tommy Furcoat'. I stood up and was in full flow with the others listening when I felt Winnie pulling at my jersey.

"Sit down," she whispered.

"But there's a lot more," I said aloud. The others began to laugh.

"We don't get up and talk like that ," Winnie hissed. Takin her word for it I sat down.

Self-expression had not yet been heard of yet in our neck of the woods and Winnie, who was shy herself, was only doing what she thought right by keeping me in line.

Infants used to stay from 9 to 4 like the rest, so I'd just about had enough of school when we started the long walk home. With the last part up-hill I really was tired when we got there. At bed time I had 'no need of rocking', as they used to say.

Next morning we set off again with Mother waving at the gate. We had gone about 50 yards when I looked back and saw she had gone in. Seized with sudden panic I turned and ran back into the house leaving Winnie to go on for fear of being late.

"I'm not going to school," was all I could say.

Mother did not reply. She just unbraced my shorts and smacked me hard on the bottom.

Then she said firmly: "Never do that again, Now go to bed."

In the long hours that followed, the shame of the indigni-

46

ty seared into my soul. And to make matters worse, it was Tuesday - wash day. I was allowed to get up at eleven, but nothing could mitigate the misery. Mother hardly spoke to me except to comment we would have to see what Father had to say.

He came home for dinner and must have been in a good mood for he said surprisingly little. But even that was small consolation. I had gained nothing. School would be waiting for me next morning - and for ever.

There were alternative roads to school; one, marginally shorter, went through Llangoed, the other past the beach at Lleiniog. For the first few years we used the latter as Winnie disliked meeting the children going to Llangoed school.

Traffic was light, the occasional horse drawn carriage or farm cart; which was a well for there were at least seven right angled bends. The most infamous was a steep hill with a low wall at the bottom and a high bank surmounted by trees that hid oncoming traffic. This had been the scene of a fatal accident The brakes on a boy's bike failed. He was projected full speed into the low wall and hurtled over the top and down into the field many feet below. His neck was broken and he died instantly.

Such events were regarded by many as 'Acts of God' and unavoidable. Yet after this tragedy some of the bank on the inside was cut away to improve the visibility.

It was my good fortune that everyone at home spent some time reading. The alphabet was then the key to learning to read, so I was taught that and someone would usually listen as I tried to make out the words in a simple primer that had found its way into the house.

A milestone in reading that I remember well was the first page in a book I managed by myself. The story was called 'Rough, the Story of a Dog'. Making out some of the words was a great struggle. Yet after that supreme effort I never had any real difficulty in reading again. Have others felt the same elation?

That I can recall the event so vividly goes to emphasize that I remember nothing of what I was taught in the infant class. Until recently I never gave this a thought and only realised it when on a visit to the Archives Office in Llangefni where I saw the old School Log Book that contained a copy of the Report of a visiting HMI in 1919.

Of the Infant Class he wrote:

"Almost the whole of one morning session was occupied by

the children of 6 to 7 years of age in adding slate arithmetic and in copying a writing exercise from the blackboard. teaching has been exceedingly formal and lifeless, and the pupils have derived little benefit from their lessons."

Comments on the other classes were hardly better. The temporary Headmaster, whom I recall as an imposingly built six-footer, had not been able to produce the Record Book and exam results from the previous year. The best that could be said was that they had made 'fairly good progress in English and Arithmetic'. Of History and Geography they had 'scarcely any grasp at all and could only give confused and unsatisfactory answers to the most simple questions'.

He had exercised ineffective control over the school and given little advice to the inexperienced and unqualified young woman in charge of the lower standards in the main classroom. Although she had been conscientious and painstaking, the progress of her pupils had been thoroughly unsatisfactory. The Report concluded that 'Quite half of the pupils now on roll are extremely backward.'

The plain fact was that the school had been badly run for years. How many children's lives had been adversely affected is impossible to say. In my family, Tillis had not won a scholarship, which, from his later achievements he should have done. Ernie, admittedly a handful, never got down to serious learning when he was there.

Jack became convinced he was incapable of academic success, partly because Father lost patience on him. He should still have been at school during my first year but opted, with the connivance of the temporary head, to go to work on a farm. In later life he could read perfectly, write a good letter, and became expert at mending watches and constructing wireless sets when broadcasting first started. Yet he could never bring himself to sit relatively easy exams that would have secured his future.

Your Loving
Brother
Teddie
14.12.18

49

7

As an infant my mind was cluttered with images of people I had heard of but never seen. They evolved mysteriously from what I had been told or had overheard grown-ups discussing; snatches of conversation about the World where a War was raging, gloomy stories about religion and frightening fairy tales. It was a world in which people, animals and spirits were either very good or very bad. And all the time I was trying to reconcile it with what I could see around me.

The two most powerful beings in this world of the mind seemed to have much in common. They were God and Miss Pritchard. I had never seen either. Yet they were ever present. God lived in the sky which was only just above the tree tops. Miss Pritchard lived in Bryn Hyfryd, a big house hardly visible behind impenetrable walls and towering trees. Compared with other houses I had seen, Bryn Hyfryd was a palace.

In my first Summer holidays, when I was six, Father began to take me to work with him. This may have been to get me out of Mother's way. But he was a firm believer in the dictum that children ought to be doing something useful lest Satan find work for their idle hands. So I had to go along with him for a morning or afternoon.

At first I was enthusiastic. It made me feel grown-up. But that soon wore off. The work I was given was, in the nature of things, monotonous - or as they say today, 'boring', a word not then in common use.

They mainly had to do with plant pots which were then all of the clay variety and heavy; carrying them from place to place, breaking up cracked ones with a hammer for crocks to cover the holes for drainage when potting up the plants. That was quite good fun for a while except they never seemed to break into the right sizes to suit Father.

Then there was the business of washing out the dirty pots. On a fine day this wasn't so bad as I could sit out in the sun. On a wet day it was sheer misery. For one thing I was left by myself in the potting shed. I stood there with a pile of dirty pots stacked inside each other, a bucket of cold water and a scrubbing brush in my hand. The door was shut but draughts whistled through all the nooks and crannies.

In no time my hands were wet, cold and dirty. The water began to trickle down my sleeves. My nose began to drip and with no way of getting at my hanky – a square piece of rag cut from an old sheet – I just had to sniffle or else resort to the sleeve of my jersey. This was strictly forbidden. But I did it with a feeling of perverse satisfaction that I was getting my own back.

After one of these wretched mornings I protested to Mother that I'd much rather stay at home. She said Father would have to decide. As I'd expected he became quite annoyed and told me how lucky I was; how boys of my age used to be sent up chimneys and down coal mines and how he'd had to do far more than the simple jobs I was asked to do when he was my age. He added that I didn't know I was born.

When I finally met Miss Pritchard it was a harrowing experience. The day was warm and sunny, the only ones the old lady, now in her seventies ventured out of her house. Father told me she was coming to look at the gardens and hearing that I was helping him, would like to see me. I felt not a little perturbed and he did nothing to make things easier by saying:

"Now I want you to give a good impression. And do speak up."

Not having had much practice in speaking up to even ordinary adults, this made me feel even more nervous.

Waiting for the old lady to appear I can only describe as what one goes through before an important interview with no great hope of getting the post. I fiddled around with what I was supposed to be doing, something to do with pots in a cold frame, and kept looking at the gravel path from the Big House where I expected her to appear. I was still caught unawares.

"Come on, she's here now," I heard Father say. I looked up and there, just distinguishable under a rose arch about ten yards away a figure was standing. I walked behind Father to the spot, feeling so overawed that the first impression I got was indistinct.

As my mind cleared it recorded a very old lady under a frilled parasol, rather tall and dressed in a good deal of flowing muslin. A wide summer hat shaded a face that was tinged with yellow and unsmiling. It was a large face, wrinkled and sagging with pendulous cheeks.

52

After Father introduced me she asked me a question about myself in a voice I remember sounding like Dame Edith Evans as Lady Bracknell. My mouth was so dry I could hardly stammer out a reply. She was evidently not impressed for she immediately went on to talk to Father about the garden while I stood there dumb.

When she had gone Father scolded. "Why didn't you speak up? I'm sure she didn't catch a word you said."

That was all very well for him. He was always at ease with the gentry because he knew the right note to strike. I never was because I never did. In fact I have to admit that striking the right note with authority was to remain a problem for some years.

But to be fair, this was only one side of my relationship with Father. We usually got on well. The best time of the day came when work was done and we set off for home. Sometimes he acted as if a weight was lifted off his mind and we would race the fifty yards between the two big gates of the stable yard. At first he used to give me a start and beat me easily. Then it got closer. He still won but each time he was getting that bit slower while I was getting faster. With time on my side the time was sure to come when I won.

"You're too fast for me now," he said ruefully smiling and looking quite pleased. Anyway, he was 55 and I was 7. In one respect I felt superior.

Those stable gates held a fascination for me. They opened in such a wide arc and the hinges were set at an angle so that they closed themselves. I used to try whenever I could to swing on them without Father or the coachman noticing.

A good time was in dry spells when the water butts at home dried up. To replenish the supply we borrowed the water carrier used for the gardens. This clumsy but invaluable conveyance was a galvanised container, the size of a large cask, swinging over two iron wheels and with iron handles supported by two legs at the front.

The water had to be drawn from a pump down beyond the stable yard which meant a haul of more than 200 yards to our house. That pump was temperamental. It used to send up air instead of water no matter how hard we pumped. The trick was to pour a can of water down from the top and then work the handle like mad. This generally made the water gush out suddenly in satisfying bursts.

With the container full it was no easy matter for Father to get the iron wheels rolling on the uphill gravelly surface.

Then there were the two big gates to be opened and shut. I'd open the first and hold it to let Father through. Knowing he would be too occupied in keeping the carrier in motion I'd have a swing on the gate as it closed. A dash then to the second gate to repeat the process. Once home the water had to be ladled with a bucket into the empty butt. Our supply was then secure for the next couple of weeks.

For drinking the water was usually boiled. But in summer we used a primitive water filter, a two gallon stone container divided into two sections with a small sponge as a filter stuffed into a hole in the centre of the divider. To work it the stone lid was lifted off the top and water poured in. It dripped through the sponge to the lower part and was drawn off for drinking with a little tap, which was the nearest we ever got to tap water.

At intervals the sponge was taken out and the accumulated sediment washed out. We were blissfully ignorant that this method of filtration had long since been condemned by medical experts as worse than useless. The sponge was more likely to harbour bacteria than to remove them. Nevertheless we managed to survive, apparently unharmed; and the water tasted as cool and fresh as none has done since.

8

Father's position a Bryn Hyfryd entitled him to some fringe benefits. One was free milk. Normally he would bring this home in a quart can when he returned for breakfast at 8. But if the milk was late I would be sent to fetch it before school.

The dairy, an integral part of the house, was approached through a wicket gate in a huge 8 feet high door set in a still higher wall that ran the length of the estate on the road side, sealing it off from intruders. Set with broken glass in concrete on top, it was so high that even a traveller on horse-back standing in his stirrups could hardly see over it.

Before reaching the dairy there was generally a hazard in the form of Miss Pritchard's pair of black pomeranians; the most aggressive, yapping, sneaky dogs I have known. As soon as my hand touched the latch they would signal their intentions with a shrill chorus of yelps. I would pass gingerly in with the chorus rising to a frenzy as the pair pranced about, sparring for an opening. Their strategy was to work their way round to my heels, a form of attack to which a boy in shorts is particularly vulnerable.

To counter this I had to keep facing them and edge slowly backwards. More than once I was tempted to kick out. But I knew that would never do. To have kicked one of Miss P's precious darlings would really have been asking for trouble. One never knew who might be watching. Fortunately, after a few yards they would give up, honour vindicated and trot back to wait for the next intruder.

Mary, the dairy maid, was a jolly buxom young woman, with rounded arms and a face as clear and smooth as the milk she poured from the pails. I would sometimes linger to watch as she turned the curiously slung barrel of a churn and listen to the milk sloshing inside. That the pats of butter on the slate slab could come from the milk, leaving the tart buttermilk that I could only drink with any pleasure on a hot summer's day, seemed miraculous to me then.

Once or twice I saw an old woman from the estate carrying on a conversation with Mary. She always wore a black shawl and was suspected of secreting the odd half pound of butter under it when Mary wasn't looking.

Many years later, Thelwal Jones, who had been one of Father's under-gardeners, told me how he once saw the old woman approaching the dairy and hid himself in the loft above. Looking down he saw her about to lay her hand on a piece of butter just as Mary turned away. He called down in sepulcral tones:

"- - - -   - - - -, I am watching you. What will you say in the Day of Judgement when all your sins are read out? Go home, woman. Go home and pray on your knees for forgiveness."

The old woman looked up apprehensively and seeing no one, beat a hasty retreat. When Thelwal came down both he and Mary, who had been suffering agonies to keep a straight face, fell about laughing.

"It was a good lark," said Thelwal. "But it had no effect on old So-and-so. She was soon back to her old tricks."

Another perk was permission to take two rows of potatoes out of a field in the Autumn. I'm not sure but this may have been a War-time concession. At all events my parents were glad of those potatoes. They lasted through the winter and helped make ends meet.

In October 1918 Father and Glyn his assistant had been given the morning off from ordinary work to do the picking. I can place the time quite accurately as it was in the week of our half-term holiday known as Teachers' Rest, which was the third week in the month. I was six and although I normally liked messing about or day-dreaming to work of any sort for some reason I was all for going along to give a hand with the potato picking.

For one thing I liked Glyn. He was a strong young man of about 20 and a good worker in spite of having one leg shorter than the other and walking with a limp. He was quiet and always looked serious. Father said he was one of the best assistants he'd ever had and was sorry he would soon be moving on to better himself. At least that's what they both thought at the time. They were not to know how the next ten years would see the big estates broken up by taxation and death duties and there would no longer be any call for gardeners.

I know that is what happened to Glyn, By 1930 he was unemployed and embittered. All the knowledge and gardening skills he had learnt were useless and would remain so.

56

We left the house at 8.30, straight after breakfast. For our mid-morning break Mother had poured boiling tea into a can, added hot milk, wrapped the can in a thick cloth to keep it warm and made up a parcel of buttered potato cakes she'd baked the night before.

As we were going out she said to me confidentially, "I've made a small one specially for you. So you'll know which is yours."

Her idea, or so I reckoned, was that being smaller than Father and Glyn, I'd only need a smaller cake. But the way she said it was as if it was something special. So I was particularly looking forward to the small potato cake.

To get to the potato field we walked diagonally across the home paddock. It was uphill and Glyn limped along wheeling the big wooden wheelbarrow with the sacks and buckets in it. The air was cold and clammy with a thick mist and the grass sodden with water droplets. Half way up we could hear the two big cart horses cropping the grass and snuffling away out of sight in the mist. It was eerie knowing they were there and not seeing them.

We passed through the five barred gate in the top corner and into the potato field. It was the highest point but still covered with mist that kept visibility down to 20 yards. I was surprised to find the potatoes lying on top of the soil. Father told me a machine pulled by a horse had turned them up.

He handed me a bucket and told me my job would be to pick up the 'chatties'. Glyn and he would take a row each picking up the big potatoes and leave the little ones, which is what he meant by 'chatties' to me. Because of my size this arrangement seemed right and proper. So in spite of the nip in the air I set to and progressed along the rows quite happily.

After a while I began to feel hungry and think about the small potato cake that was waiting in the basket at the side of the field. I'd no idea of the time till at last Father took out his watch from his waistcoat pocket and said to Glyn;

"It's near enough to 10 now. We'll take a break."

We sat down on the sacks while Father poured out the tea into enamel mugs, then opened the packet of potato cakes. As I watched I had to swallow a couple of times in anticipation, He held out the packet to Glyn first and I could see my small potato cake sitting on top. To my horror Glyn took it. For a moment I was speechless. Then I blurted out:

"But the little one was for me."

57

Oh, don't be silly, boy. They all taste the same," Father said in his no nonsense voice.

It was too late anyway, Glyn had already taken a bite out of my potato cake and was looking quite guilty. Father held out the packet to me. I took the top one and began to eat. It nearly choked me. It was no use him saying they all tasted the same. I knew it was nowhere near as nice as the small one would have been.

We were soon back at work though my heart had gone out of it . All the potatoes were gathered by 11.30. The mountains were now just visible across the Straits in the pale autumn sun. The cows were congregated at the lower end of the field below. The grey bull stood by itself near the wire fence looking disdainfully at us.

The two full sacks and the chatties I'd put in a smaller one were loaded on to the wheelbarrow. With Glyn wheeling it we started off home. They piled up the potatoes at the back of the shed and put the sacks over them to keep out the frost. They'd both forgotten all about the small potato cake.

But I hadn't. I told Mother, expecting sympathy. She said:

"What a shame. Never mind. I'll make you another next time and tell Father about it beforehand."

The never was a next time. With the War over that was the last year we had free potatoes. It was nice of her to promise. But I could tell by the way she talked she had no idea what a disapointment I'd had.

At the time I never paused to consider the vast amount of time and energy Father must have expended in stocking and maintaining all those flower beds, fruit trees and greenhouses with such a variety of plants. For he had the assistance of one apprentice who invariably departed for a more lucrative post once he had been trained.

He managed, of course, by working long hours and with the complete dedication of the old-time gardener. In summer he would return to work after tea, often carrying on until twilight and regarding this as normal. Apart from Saturday afternoon, Sunday, Christmas Day and, after the War, Bank Holidays, he had no regular time off. Even on these free days he would turn in to do essential watering and adjusting temperatures. If he happened to travel a mile or so from home, unless his assistant was there, he would be on tenterhooks, keeping an eye on the weather, ready to hurry back to adjust the lights in the three large greenhouses and the cold frames.

58

The greenhouses, all single-span against high brick walls, were designed to accommodate almost every variety of plant. The hot-house, about a third of 20 yards of glass facing south, was sectioned off by a glass partition at the end nearest the stove house. There tropical plants and ferns grew in a steamy heat produced by hot water that surged through double rows of 4 inch pipes and regular hand spraying.

Beyond this the houses ranged from the warm with its African violets, poinsettias, colleoses and huge begonias to the cool where calceolarias, cinerarias and the like were set out in banks of glorious colour.

Then there was the vinery from which the stems of the vines, wrapped with sacking, disappeared through holes in the low brick wall below the glass into the bed of rich, dark brown soil. That empty bed was at first a mystery to me. It seemed such a waste with no plants growing in it. Father explained at last that vines were 'hungry feeders'. If anything else was grown in the soil it would rob them of nourishment so the bunches of grapes would be smaller.

Those vines were certainly well fed. Apart from the layer of horse dung with straw on top, they were supplied with regular doses of liquid manure from the cows in the shippon. This stinking stuff had to be dragged in a water carrier half a mile, across the field, up the hill and along a gravelled drive. A double layer of sacking was tied over the top of the container to stop the liquid splashing out. But as the sacking became soaked by the jolting, the stench rose high and pervasive.

Father warned me to be careful: "Don't get that stuff on your clothes or you'll have it for a week."

I held my nose but he only grinned and added: "That's nothing yet. In a few weeks time it will be really ripe."

I thought it strange that the manure's potency should be gauged by its stink. It was left to mature before the appropriate doses, carefully diluted, were applied to the weeded and carefully raked bed over the vine roots.

Like the hot house, a part of the vinery nearest the stove was sealed of with a glass partition and an interior door. Here, trapped in the maximum heat were Father's pride and joy, the greenish muscatels. His enthusiasm for them puzzled me. The black ones with their bluish sheen looked so much nicer. But there it was; for him the muscatel was the prince of grapes.

As all the stoves relied on gravity for circulating the hot water, they were housed in brick built sheds with floors well below ground level. For the vinery it was a good three feet down and large enough to hold an ample supply of coke shovelled in through a trap door at the side.

On winter nights, at 7 o'clock, Father would light up his hurricane lantern and go on his rounds stoking up the stoves for the night. Sometimes I went with him. And if he had been reading us an adventure story by Stevenson or Ballantyne my excitement would be all the more intense as we stepped out into the darkness. I would clutch tight his work-hardened hand for reassurance.

One night a high wind lashed the bare branches of the trees, whistling shrilly. As I looked up at the clouds scudding across the moon the earth seemed to reel under my feet.

On another the air was frosty, the sky star-lit but with no moon. Outside the constantly moving little circle of light cast by the swinging lantern the hedgerows and the black trees stood stark and motionless.

An owl screeched as we left the house. We walked down the road and into the stable yard, our boots grinding the gravel surface. As we passed through the lower gate another owl screeched louder still from the conifers ahead. Then a rustling in the branches and a faint whistling sound.

"He's got something," Father said.

With a tingle of fear I held on tighter to his hand.

We made our way along the turns of the path towards the vinery, the farthest away of the green houses. Father lifted the latch of the low door of the stovehouse and went down the stone steps made awkwardly steep to conserve space. As I followed, the sudden heat and acrid fumes from the open door caught at my throat, taking my breath away. But Father just went on opening the top and bottom doors of the stove to rake down the ashes. The fire glowed and more intense fumes mixed with fine ash filled the enclosed space for he had told me to shut the stove house door to keep in the heat. I held my breath and closed my eyes tight to ease the pain.

When I opened them he had taken up the heavy wooden mallet to smash up the coke. Then he began stoking up for the night, each shovelful adding black spurts of smoke to the dust and fumes.

At last it was all done. I climbed the stone steps and with intense relief gulped in the cold clear air with a curious sense of achievement as though I had survived some ordeal.

Neither of the other stove houses was so fume-filled. Although as big, the stove for the hot house was only a foot

below ground level and not so enclosed. The third was smaller and only used for background heat. I'm sure Father had no
conception of the risk he was taking with those deadly coke
fumes when he paid his nightly visits to the vinery. Yet it
seems not to have harmed him in any way.

He had no serious illness throughout his long life and I
cannot remember his staying off work for a minor one. Yet
he often complained about his digestion and was kept going
on four small meals a day, at 8, 12, 4 and 8, as regular as
the clock.

He was a worrier so long as he had the responsibilities of
family and work. He worried about the garden with pests
like aphis on the roses and red spider on the vines. He worried about the weather, which was nearly always 'abnormal'.
He suspected old David Jones the butler of telling lies about
him to Miss Pritchard.

He worried about the War, the state of the Country and
the Empire. On Lloyd George he was ambivalent. While he
detested his politics he once walked all the way to Caernarvon to hear the great orator speak. The man had admittedly
brought in Old Age Pensions, 'the Lloyd George' as he used
to call it, but he was a Liberal and therefore suspect. As for
the Socialists, they were out to ruin the Country. The very
thought of them made his blood boil.

His blood used to boil unexpectedly and for no apparent
reason that I could see. Mother bore the brunt of it with her
usual passive resignation. Perhaps that made him worse. His
tirades used to upset me when I was small. I used to hate
him then and wish I could take Mother away out of it.

Now I think it was not all so black and white. If Mother
had been able to stand up for herself and not adhered so lit-
erally to the 'honour and obey' part of her marriage, he
may have been more restrained.

There was one thing in his favour though. He never carried
a grievance for long. In fact he would change his mood with
remarkable suddenness - like turning off the gas.

One Saturday he had been at it laying down the law just
before setting out on his usual jaunt to Beaumaris. As he
went through the gate Edith was standing by the window
looking out pensively at the road. She started smiling and
said: "Just come and look at this."

We crowded to the window and there was Father chatting
away genially to a passing acquaintance.

"Look at him," said Edith. "You wouldn't think it was the
same man."

Some years later Mother confided that when they were first married she used to cry when he got annoyed over nothing, but she'd become hardened. "He can't hurt me the same now," she said. By that time though Father was in semi-retirement with fewer worries. The fires were burning down, his flash point was lower.

Once, when I was a teenager I ventured to criticise him to her. Mother flew loyally to his defence. "He's been a good father to you. You must never forget that."

She was right. It is not only the material side I have to thank him for. He had a great love for the written word, and in particular the 19th Century novelists. It gave him a retreat from the harsher realities of life and without it I believe he would not have lasted so long. Fortunately for me he had the urge to share his enthusiasm with others. He was like an actor who rises above his own character to portray another. He was not a good conversationalist. But he read fluently and dramatically enough to communicate his enthusiasm to his unsophisticated audience - Mother, Winnie and myself.

He had not read to the older members of the family, a fact they sometimes regretted, and seems to have developed the habit from reading to Mother for half an hour after his mid-day meal. He still carried on with this and sometimes used the occasion for trial runs of books suitable for Winnie and me.

He found the chapter in Conan Doyle's 'Sir Nigel',where the young knight breaks in a wild horse so exciting that he read it to us the same evening. We begged him to read the whole book. He did and followed it with 'The White Company'. Eventually we must have heard all that author's works including the Sherlock Holmes and Brigadier Gerard stories.

His taste had not been cramped by literary criticism. If he came upon a book he liked he read it. He then read all he could get of that author's books, borrowing from the lending library in the Chemist's shop at Beaumaris at 2d a book or from some other source. We had most of Dickens, (his favourite), Stevenson and selections from George Eliot, Dumas and Victor Hugo, not to mention writers of adventure stories like Ballantyne, Fennimore Cooper, Baroness Orczy and Stanley Weyman.

He would read for three quarters of an hour by the clock,then stop. If he'd come to an exciting part we begged for more, he occasionally relented. He would never read the week-day book on Sunday. He once tried to fill the time by reading us a serial from Mother's 'Sunday Companion' in which the hero was a parson. It was so awful and we showed so little interest that he quietly dropped it.

He seldom read aloud from the Bible but could quote from it to fit the occasion. "Remember thy Creator in the days of thy youth", was one he never tired of repeating. I did not follow his advice. But in later life it led me to read and learn by heart that most beautiful evocation of old age which follows.

Above all it was the characters from Dickens that captured his imagination. Sam Weller, Mr Micawber, Uriah Heap and many others were so alive to him that they almost became members of the family.

9

The War was woven into the fabric of our lives. Mother and Father talked earnestly about it every day. I was used to hearing such words as 'our boys', France, Germany, the trenches and the Somme.

News of it filtered down to us in rumours and delayed reports in the papers. My parents feared the worst but with trust that God was on our side, they developed a fatalistic stoicism.

To me, like so much that was happening it was all very confusing. Where was the War? When I asked, someone said it was in France and pointed vaguely to the front of the house. So I thought it must be behind the trees on the other side of the road.

I knew it was not at the back of the house. The camp was there, just beyond the Vicarage field and out of sight. But on a calm day bugle calls came echoing faintly. A gun was fired at certain times of the day. Father set his pocket watch by it as he started for work at 1pm.

Columns of khaki clad men came marching along the road. Edith had made me a little uniform out of one that Tillis had left behind when he was commissioned. At the distant sound of marching I rushed to the gate. There was no sign of the men yet. But as the steady beat rose louder and louder the khaki figures swung into view round the bend in the road. Small at first the grew larger with every step till the sound of their iron shod boots reached a crescendo. My big moment had come.

I'd stand to attention and give the salute. Most of the men looked ahead. But some would smile and wink and pass comments. I cannot remember what they said now. But there was something about a mascot and for a brief moment I was in a heaven of excitement and joy.

By 1917 I had found out the War was not just behind the trees because I went further than that to school. It had receded behind the mountains on the far side of the Straits. One day at the beach I thought I could hear the sound of guns. But Winnie told me it was only the blasting at the stone quarry further along the coast at Penmon.

64

The pleasure of going out to salute soon waned and I used to watch the men marching with little more than curiousity. Then one day in early September we knew that a larger body of men was going to march past. They were being drafted to the Front.

It was evening and all the family were waiting to stand outside to wave goodbye. As soon as they left the camp we knew they were on their way. The strains of 'Pack up your troubles in your old kit bag', played by the Regimental Band came wafted on the breeze. As the leading column hove into view the song had changed.

"Keep the home fires burning
While your hearts are yearning.
Though the boys are far away
They dream of home.
There's a silver lining
Through the dark clouds shining,
Turn the dark clouds inside out
Till the boys come home."

How bravely they sang. How wildly we waved, right until the last man had disappeared round the bend in the road. In all the excitement I had seen Mother trying vainly to smile. As we walked in the tears were coursing down her cheeks and I felt overawed by the contrasting silence which had fallen over all.

About this time we had some postcards with pen and ink cartoons of the officers in the Camp. They must have disappeared with the break-up of our home. But memories of the sketches were revived in 1979 when I visited a veteran of the Camp, Miss Sally Williams at her home in Beaumaris. Miss Williams had worked for two years in the cook-house before joining the WAACs and at 88 she retained clear and happy memories of those years.

Her mementos included a collection of postcard photos of the Camp and the men together with 12 of the cartoons of the officers and one of the CO's dog, Peter. The name of the artist was Bernard W Handley. On further enquiries I found that Handley had been sporting cartoonist on the ROCHDALE TIMES, had contributed to Manchester papers and after volunteering in 1915, his sketches had appeared regularly in the Royal Engineer's Magazine, SAPPER.

He must have been in the draft I had seen marching past in September 1917 for that was the month he arrived in

65

France. For a short while he continued to sketch with his usual ironic humour the men and the scenes of desolation around him. Then, on 30th October, only a few weeks after he arrived, his time ran out. He was killed while asleep in the trenches.

Miss Williams kindly gave me the cartoons and photos. Copies are now in the Archives at Llangefni. The cartoons I have mounted in a frame, a treasured memorial to the artist and those sad times.

The Camp, named Kingsbridge after the stone bridge that spans the stream, was I suppose like thousands of others that mushroomed in the War years. But for the men from many parts of the Country and the Empire who passed through it and for the local people, it became symbolic of the War. Even for me the strands of memory stretching back nearly 70 years intertwine with the present with unusual poignancy. I have wondered why this should be.

Its origins were not auspicious. They began in 1902 when the site was chosen for a tented Summer camp for the militia, which included infantry and the Royal Anglesey Royal Engineers. The latter were taught 'smithy work, carpentry, bridge building and musketry.

The permanent staff was based in Beaumaris. They used to go far afield on recruiting drives and could not be too particular as to the character of their recruits. CSM Frank Shipperlee, a Boer War veteran and a fine example of the 'back bone of the British Army', had Stockport as his preserve. Frank had been with his wife and young family at the Seige of Ladysmith. His son Fred who was 81 when I saw him a few years ago, told me he was a year old when the Seige began and was the only baby out of 34 to survive. He was able to sketch the lay-out of Kingsbridge Camp without hesitation after all those years.

While popular with the inn-keepers at Beaumaris, the militia were feared and detested by the local farmers for the damage they caused to animals, crops and fences when on their way home from the pubs on pay days. The farmers complained to the Commandant who solved the problem by witholding most of the men's pay till the end of the course.

With the outbreak of War radical changes took place in both the Camp and the personnel. Hutments with all the appendages of a permanent camp were soon erected. Its role was switched to the exclusive training of Engineers which meant an influx of volunteers from all walks of life.

66

Filling the bucket
R.A.R.E. Sports

67

Drunkenness virtually disappeared and farmers ceased to complain. The Camp became an important economic and social part of the community.

Most of the staff I remember as household names. After the War many settled in and around Beaumaris, adding to the number of non Welsh names in the town. Included were Bannister, Clayton, Shipperlee and Sloan.

The Camp had a few lorries that trundled along at an alarming speed of over 20 miles an hour. Like most other things they were made to last: wheels with thick wooden spokes and solid rubber tyres, curved strips of metal to serve as mudguards and lamps like those on old horse-drawn coaches. They had no doors or windscreen, though strips of canvas could be clipped on to keep out some of the weather.

But the most common means of transport for goods and sometimes men were great springless, spine-jolting wagons drawn by teams of two or four mules. These conveyances were as dangerous as modern traffic and certainly more frightening on the narrow, uneven surfaces of country roads.

One morning in the Spring of 1918 Winnie and I were on our way to school. We had passed the beach and were in the narrow lane that ran in a curve almost following the shore line before turning sharply inland to the left. We heard the familiar clatter of hoofs behind us and got on to the grass at the side to let whatever it was pass by.

As the sound drew nearer it increased to a gallop as a wagon drawn by four mules came swinging round the curve, the driver standing up and tugging savagely at the reins. We flung ourselves into the hedge as the mules then the wagon, bouncing and swaying went hurtling past.

Seconds later, quite unable to take the corner, the mules went crashing through the thick-set hedge and came to a halt with the wagon half on the road and half in the field. For a moment there was a lull and I suspect it was a moot point whether the mules, the driver or ourselves were most frightened; the only sounds the snorting and uneasy jostling of the mules.

Then the driver came suddenly to life, cursing at the top of his voice and flogging the mules on into the field. He tugged viciously at their bits, bringing them back in a circle to the gap and through on to the road. They rattled away, the driver still cursing, leaving us to stare at the crushed and broken remains of the hedge.

I think what shocked me most was the driver's cursing.

71

Swearing was not then the normal currency of language and what we did hear was usually of the mildest sort. How times have changed.

For some time I had wanted to see the gun at the Camp being fired. One Saturday morning Edith said she would give Winnie and me a treat by taking us there to see it at one o'clock. So as soon as dinner was over, off we went.

The gun, which was really a cannon, stood on a slab of concrete just inside the big gate of the main entrance. It was much smaller than I had expected, never having been so near to it before. Still, I was impressed by its polished brass that shone in the sunlight.

After we'd stood near the open gate for a few minutes a tall, fair haired soldier came up to the cannon and waved to us. Edith waved back. We watched as he bent over the cannon, did something to it and stepped back, holding a cord. He looked intently at his watch for what seemed a long time then pulled the cord. There was a deafening bang and a puff of white smoke.

The tall soldier came over to the gate for a few minutes, and talked with Edith. After that we started off home with Edith looking very pleased with life. It did not occur to me that Edith was really giving herself a treat by taking us to see the gun.

Over the next few weeks the tall soldier, a South African, came to our house regularly for supper. Edith was 'walking out' with him and used to refer to him as 'Long Legs'. Then he left for the Front and she was upset. She received letters at irregular intervals. But after a while it was silence and she never knew what happened to him.

Early in 1919 most of the troops were being demobbed or moved to other camps and German prisoners-of-war moved in. The NORTH WALES CHRONICLE reported on June 20th that "Fifty German prisoners-of-war are employed at the camp filling trenches, etc. On Tuesday they marched through the streets of Beaumaris for exercise and their appearance created much interest."

Came the Summer holidays and I watched them marching down to Lleniog beach for a swim and was surprised to find they looked so like 'our boys' except for their dark uniform. Most were able to swim and I never saw so many heads bobbing in the water. Two particularly good swimmers almost disappeared out of sight. I began to think they were trying

72

to escape. But when a shrill whistle was blown they turned back and made for the beach. I wondered why they did not carry on to the other side of the Straits, where, in my imagination they would have been free.

On August 29th they must have gone; for the CHRONICLE reported the camp's closure "to a nominal establishment". The material loss to the town and locality, it said, would be considerable. But apart from this there would be a feeling of regret for the close attachment that existed between the hundreds of men who had passed through the camp and the townsfolk. All that was possible had been done willingly to make the stay of the 'boys' as agreeable as circumstances permitted. Valued friendships had been formed - - - .

CHEER OH

TO BLIGHTY

GOOD WISHES From 8709 Sapper Bernard W. Handley.
A Depot Coy. RA R Engineers, Kingsbridge Camp,
XMAS · 1916   Beaumaris, ANGLESEY.

CARTOONS OF OFFICERS AT KINGSBRIDGE CAMP DRAWN BY BERNARD W HANDLEY.

The following comments were written about some of the officers on the cards the artist sent home and are reproduced by kind permission of his brother Alan T Handley.

CAPTAIN W A YOCKNEY. Quite one of the best officers I have met. He has always a 'good morning' when coming to the drawing office for the sketch to be drawn. He has a terrible hate of the R A R E Band and is always off when he hears the drum beat. It was he who said at the opening of the YWCA, 'I'm afraid it's the leg on the other boot'.

CAPTAIN AND ADJUTANT DARBY DOWMAN. Quite a good sort and of course potters about with the Colonel like a dog trotting with his master. Acts as a sort of general secretary for the Colonel and his chief duty seems to call out on General parade, 'All present, Sir.' He always walks about with his hands in his pockets and his pipe in his mouth. You would miss his pipe before his nose if either was missing.

(PETER was the Colonel's dog.)

LIEUT R W B OWENS. Quite one of the most sporting officers of the R A R E. He was in a high position in the banking line and comes from Liverpool, living in Waterloo. He gets the wind up very quickly but after all is quite harmless and wouldn't do a chap a bad turn. He was very upset to find he generally stands with his toes turned in.

LIEUT E L ROBERTS. The chief officer of the musketry business - the art of shooting Germans and generally guarding bridges with pieces of hot lead. He made an awful noise about his breeches but the Adjutant said I hadn't drawn them half bad enough.

LIEUT AND QM A E HENDERSON. A very straightforward man who has always a pleasant word for everybody. He has most of the general supply of the camp to see to. Another point to note about Lieut Henderson is that he has rather a nice duaghter.

(MAJOR T FANNING EVANS was of a well-known Anglesey family.)

(LIEUT H REID was Officer in Charge of Field Works. Note the poor cat.)

Major. T. FANNING. EVANS.

Capt. W. A. YOCKNEY.

Capt. & A. DARBY. DOWMAN.

PETER.

Lieut. H. REID.
Officer in Charge
F.

Lieut R.W.B. OWENS

Lieut E.L. ROBERTS

Lieut & Qr Mr A.E. HENDERSON

10

After those wasted years in the infants, things took a turn for the better. The school came under the control of a firm hand.

Mr Richard Thomas, (Dick Tom, as he was sometimes referred to when out of earshot), was a tall. athletically built man with strong features, a high forehead and a rather sallow complexion. His eyes, by which children instinctively weigh up their chances, were set well apart and his gaze was direct and unwavering. He came with a reputation for excessive caning, which, in my experience was not justified.

He arrived in May 1919 and by the next term, when I moved up to the class of his assistant, Miss Katy Matthews, in the main classroom, she was evidently working to a proper syllabus. From now on I made steady progress in the basics, including the arithmetical tables which we loved to chant in unison at odd moments. With the Head teaching the top class at the other end of the room and under threat of being sent to him, we were on our best behaviour most of the time.

Although '12 parcels of requisites', that included some exercise books, pens, pencils and rulers arrived in September, several of the big boys having been sent to carry them all the way from Llangoed, most writing and sums were still done on slates. At the time I had no thought of where the slates and their pencils came from, though obviously, with the slate quarries across the Straits at Llanberis, they would have been made locally. But I would have been surprised to know that there was a small factory tucked out of sight behind the gas-works at Beaumaris, that was turning out the slate pencils. They actually managed to produce one that did not squeak. This must have happened just before the slates disappeared from schools for we never had one.

How I hated those slates. The filthy and unhygienic habit of spitting on them and wiping with the sleeve was used by some boys. It made me feel physically sick. It must have been possible to insisted that water and rags were used. But I suppose old habits died hard and as the only source of water was a pump at the roadside opposited the entrance to the boy's yard, this was some excuse.

The pump, incidentally, was the sole supply of water for the school, including the staff and the caretaker's house. It was later replaced by a button operated jet with a thick metal cup attached by a chain though this was rarely used.

The lesson in Miss M's class that sticks most in my memory used to come at the end of a winter's day. As the slates, books, pens and pencils were being collected and stacked away in the cupboards by the monitors, we would sit upright with arms folded. When all was ready Miss M would call out in turn the names of the ones sitting up straightest, who would take their places by the fire-guard, glowing with warmth and pride. So it went on till all were lined up. The order of precedence must have been quite arbitrary, yet none of us thought it unfair, accepting out place with equanimity.

Miss M now sat down at the other end of the fire-guard and the game began. The first in line was given a word to spell. If he failed, it was passed to the next and the one who got it correct took his place. So it went down the line with the best spellers moving towards the fire - a double honour. I suspect that no greater incentive to spell correctly has ever been devised than the prospect of standing near a warm fire on a cold winter's day.

May 28th 1920 stands out as a golden day. It was my 8th birthday and Mother promised to bring down a picnic tea and meet us on Lleiniog beach on the way home. From the moment I woke that morning the sun shone with not a cloud in the sky.

Winnie, now with the top class, presented a note from Mother to the Head asking that we be allowed to leave at 3.30. He agreed of course. The morning routine was as dull as ever but my mind was soaring above it all. Through the afternoon I kept glancing up at the high windows for clouds in the blue sky.

No sign of clouds - just a nagging doubt -would the Head remember? I was in no position to remind him and Winnie would not dare. After playtime I knew all would be well. Mr T took out his pocket watch and placed it with its chain on the front of his tall desk.

On the dot of 3.30 he told us we could go. No chant of 'Happy Birthday to you' from the class. That was never done. Just the shadow of a smile from Mr T and the studied looks of unconcern from the rest to hide their envy.

Then out into the warm sun and the hurried half-walk, half-run along the dusty road with its angular turns to the beach. We never doubted Mother would come, only whether she would be there first. Round the last bend and there she was, sitting on the grass by the little stone bridge over the stream, a basket beside her, looking out over the blue waters of the Straits.

A cloth was laid ready on the grass and the tea set out. Home-made bread with farm butter and strawberry jam. Tea from a can that had been wrapped in a white cloth to keep it warm. And a cake, marzipaned and iced with Happy Birthday in red.

The little stream, partly dammed by the sand washed up by the incoming tide had formed a pool just below the bridge. Here and there small fish flipped out of the water snapping the flies as they skimmed the surface. We looked on as we ate in lazy contentment, now and then tossing in a pebble to watch the ripples spread outwards until they disappeared into the imagination.

Tea over we were all eyes for an historic event, the first voyage between Liverpool and Bangor of 'La Marguerite' the paddle steamer after years of transporting troops to France. At 4.30, against the back-drop of the mountains she came, slowly like th proud old lady she was, chugging her way from Beaumaris towards the channel between Puffin Island and Penmon Point. Bound for Llandudno and Liverpool she seemed for us to carry all the romance of a voyage round the world. Perhaps it was only fancy but we thought we could just hear the chunking of the paddles wafted over the calm silvery waters of the Straits.

"Now, wait for the waves," said Mother, And sure enough as the white wake from the paddles widened into a great 'V' the waves came curling on to the pebbles in a flurry of activity. One - two - three - - we counted until they subsided into ripples again with hardly a fleck of foam.

Soon we heard the clop, clop of a horse and turned to see a man and a young woman alighting from a trap. They led the pony through a gate into the field behind us then took out a milk churn and two pails and stools. Leaving the pony to crop the grass they each went to one of the cows that munched contentedly as they set down the stools and started to milk.

How permanent they looked. How rooted in time. How soon they would become a fleeting memory of a vanished age.

When the last pailful had been poured into the churn, it

it was time to be going. We had no watch but the chill in the air and the lengthening shadows told us it must be near to 6 o'clock. We gathered together the picnic remains and began the leisurely walk home. It was uphill most of the way and when we reached the door I felt a little sad the day was almost over. I was 8 and had begun to sense that pleasure, like the pendulum's swing, stays in one place for only a short time.

The following August Mr T's son, Wynn, was transferred to the school. He became my closest friend and we had some happy times together. Wynn had a facial resemblance to his father though he never approached him in height. He was shorter than I but sturdier and stronger, In wrestling for a throw, the accepted mode of contest, he could put me on my back with precision. At first this erked me and I once tried to catch him unawares. The advantage was short-lived. In a few seconds I was on my back, doubly mortified at having cheated and failed.

In the holidays we sometimes wandered about the nearby countryside. Mostly it was aimless but occasionally we made plans.

Once we determined to trace the stream that flows under Kingsbridge to its source. We got quite excited about the idea, seeing it as an adventure into the unknown. We imagined that somewhere in the middle of Anglesey the stream began as a tiny trickle along the ground, no larger than a drop of rain from a downspout. We pictured the moment when we reached the spot as vividly as did the Victorian explorers in search of the source of the Nile.

At 9 one morning we met at the Bridge and, fortified with the inevitable packet of jam sandwiches for the day's trek, set out along the side of the stream. It had rained overnight so the going was heavy. Within a hundred yards we were up to the ankles in mud. One of my feet sank so deep I could hardly pull it out. The wet began to seep over the top of the boot and ooze down inside. Still, we knew that explorers would not be deterred by such small set-backs and plodded on.

After a while our hearts began to sink, at least mine did. Explorers did not have to answer to their parents for the state they arrived home in. Not only that, we began to find problems that had not entered out minds at the planning stage. We had thought of the banks of the stream as a sort of public right of way. Now we could see a farmhouse in the

80

distance There were hoofmarks in the mud where cows and horses had come down to drink. And farmers, as we knew from experience had a rooted and unreasonable dislike of boys crossing their land. Neither of us voiced these fears, our intercourse being confined to exclamations of annoyance as we squelched through the mud.

We climbed a fence and started along the side of a field. The going was easier but we kept a sharp lookout and were relieved there were no signs of a farmer. Then we saw something that stopped us in our tracks. At the far end of the field cattle were grazing and between us and them, not more than 50 yards away was a black bull.

It had seen us too and was walking in our direction with its nose up sniffing the air. That was enough. We were back over the fence in record time. The bull trotted up and snorted

We grinned at each other, glad the fence was a strong one. "That's it then," said Wynn. "Can't go any further."

"I know," I said, feeling relieved. "Let's go back to the beach."

We knew the way now and instead of squelching through the mud, walked boldly back to Kingsbridge on the fields, but still ready to run for it if we saw a farmer. Over the bridge then and down to the footpath on the other side that wound through the woods beside the tinkling stream.

We came to a wooden hut, once used for storing tools, where only a few weeks before a minor tragedy had occurred. A man from the Village had gone in and disturbed an owl that was dozing inside. Before he realised what was happening it flew at his face screeching. He'd lost an eye.

We hesitated then pushed the creaking door open slowly, peering in through our fingers held over our eyes. There was nothing but bits of wood and rubbish inside so we went on to the road at the corner where the boy had fallen off his bike to his death, and down to Lleniog beach. There we took off our soggy boots and stockings and washed them in the stream, dabbling our feet in the water. Patches of sun were coming through the clouds so we put them out to dry and ate our sandwiches although it was only 11 o'clock.

We'd both been reading a story about some boys who had escaped from an island on a raft, and looking at the stream flowing strongly after the rain gave me an idea.

"Let's make a raft and sail it down from Kingsbridge to the sea."

We talked about it for a while and decided it would be

made of logs tied together with ropes. We thought about an anchor but as we could see no way of getting one decided a big stone on a rope would have to do.

Wynn said, "We'll have to keep to the middle of the stream going under the bridges or we'll get out heads bashed in."

We both thought this very funny and had a good laugh.

I said, "If we get this far we might as well go into the sea a bit."

"If it's not too rough," said Wynn.

I agreed. "We'd better not go too far either. Not the first time anyway."

Our stockings and boots were still damp. But we put them on and walked slowly home, still full of the raft idea.

Thoughts of drifting down the river, that's how I was now seeing the stream, with Wynn and me on board filled my mind for the rest of the day and I could hardly get to sleep at night for thinking of it.

Next morning I got down to the practical side of looking for logs. Not one was to be found. There was no rope either, only pieces of thick string for tying parcels that Mother kept in a bag for future use.

Wynn came along in the afternoon looking cheerful.

I've got an idea," he said.

"About the raft?"

"No. That's a dead loss. We havn't got the logs. Anyway, how'd we get it down to the river?"

"What's this idea, then?"

"We'll have to get some horse manure first. There's plenty on the road. I just looked. And some brown paper and string. Got any?"

I took the bits of string I'd collected for the raft out of my pocket and said I could get the paper from the house.

Wynn explained his idea. "We'll make the manure into a parcel and leave it on the road as if someone dropped it. Then we'll hide and see what happens."

I went in and when Mother wasn't looking took a piece of brown paper from where she kept the sheets that had come round parcels in the post, all neatly folded. When I got out Wynn had the manure on a piece of slate. It was fairly dry and not too messy. We tipped some into the brown paper, moulded into a neat parcel shape and tied it up tight.

Placing it at the side of the road we went into the garden and lay face down against the bank with our heads below the little hedge on top so we could see what was happening.

Several vehicles went by, then we could hear footsteps. A

middle-aged woman appeared on her way home to Llangoed. She stopped by the parcel, had a quick look round, picked it up and popping it into her basket, hurried off.

"Oh, hell!" said Wynn.

We knew she'd get an unpleasant surprise but that was only half the fun.

"We'll just have to make another," I said. "And a bigger one this time so they can't carry it off so easily."

We made up the new parcel with care and took up our stations again. Soon a man we knew came along on his bike weaving a little as if he'd had a few drinks. He saw the parcel, dismounted jerkily and picked it up. When he got to the contents he puckered up his brows and cast his eyes on the hedge. I don't think he saw us but he said loudly:

"Come out you little buggers. Let me have a good look at you."

We put our heads up.

"I ought to tan your bloody hides," he said. Then his face broke into a grin.

"Please don't break it up." said Wynn in Welsh. "We want to try again."

The man twisted up his face wryly and after a moment's hesitation put the paper and its contents down on the grass.

"OK, then," he said and, shaking his head, mounted his bike and went weaving off.

The next to come I knew only by sight but Wynn whispered he was a big man in the Chapel. He certainly looked the part, heavily built and stern looking, he wore a black suit and a dark trilby hat. Like the others before him he stopped and looked around before picking up the parcel. He weighed it in his hand and had another look around, then gave way to curiousity and began to open it. When he got to the contents his face went livid.

Wynn and I looked at each other and the urge to giggle became uncontrollable. We let out subdued sniggers and tried to cover them with fits of coughing. The game was up. We stood on the bank, still trying to stifle the laughing while the man told us in Welsh exactly what he thought of us. He also said he was going to tell Wynn's father.

Theat really brought us to our senses. We decided it was time to try something else, and went down to Fryars beach to see who could skim flat stones along the surface of the water the most times.

Our school life was punctuated by outbreaks of childhood

diseases. This was regarded as part of our education - an essential preparation for life. I caught whooping cough, mumps and measles in that order. Chicken pox I missed. Like J K Jerome who perused a Medical Dictionary and found he had every desease except house-maid's knee, I felt this to be 'an invidious reservation'.

My parents were concerned only at the severity of the desease. They saw it as a milestone on life's road and had no fears about after effects. Unpleasant for us and inconvenient for them, but having survived we were innoculated for life.

We took the cue from our elders. If we caught it we were glad of the extra attention. If not there was a bonus for the schools were closed for three to five weeks as a means of restricting the spread.

Winnie and I had whooping cough at the same time which pleased Mother as she got it over at one go. Winnie suffered more than I did. At times she coughed herself blue in the face and came frighteningly near to suffocation. Mother said this was because she had a short neck and I had a longer one.

A year later I had mumps by myself. Apart from the pain when eating, mostly bread and milk, I remember Mother asking with a smile:

"Would you like to see what you look like?"

She gave me a hand mirror. Horror! Could that bloated, mishapen face really be mine? Until reassured I thought that was how I was going to look for the rest of my life.

I caught measles when I was eight. It was the only occasion thought serious enough to call in old Dr Jones from Beaumaris. A sprightly little man with a brusque manner he was decidedly eccentric. To Mother's embarrassment, Father used to enjoy telling a story about the good doctor whose surgery was in Church Street. One Sunday morning as he was setting out on a visit the church bells were ringing and when he opened his door he saw that a dog had 'left its card' on the step. Hopping mad, he kicked it away and shocked several passing church-goers by saying loudly: "This bloody town. It's nothing but church bells and dog shit."

On his first visit I was barely conscious. A few days later when I was well enough to sit up I was puzzled to see the numbers 105 and 101 written in pencil on the wall paper beside the bed. Mother explained that 105 meant I had been delirious with a high temperature and was now getting back to normal.

The days of convalescence were quite pleasant as I was

receiving more attention than usual. For a few days I was confined to bed. I felt little inclination to read but someone would drop in from time to time to read to me. Mostly I was content to lie thinking.

The window was too high to see anything but the sky, the clouds and the sun before it set. I made regular surveys of the wallpaper. It was a flowered pattern and had been badly matched at some of the joins. I did not think of this as a mistake. It seemed an essential and permanent part of the room. It had been there since I was born, since time began. I was in a dream-like state. Nothing would ever change, I told myself. I was a child. Grown-ups were grown-ups. They talked about their childhood but that was long, long ago. They would stay as grown-ups. I would stay a child - -.

I closed my eyes. My body swelled up and filled the room. It was not alarming for there was no pain. I assumed it was all part of the measles, which presumably it was. When I opened my eyes, everything came slowly back to normal. For many years after the sensation would come back unexpectedly as I lay in bed and closed my eyes. It went on intermittently right into my early twenties, when it disappeared entirely. I think of it as a pattern on the brain that was erased by time like the writing on an old document. I never thought of mentioning it to anyone - till now.

Strangely for such an out of the way place as Penmon there were three coloured children on the roll when I began. The story went that their father fought in the South African War and married a Boer. On this ironic misinformation there is no need to comment.

The one who stands out in my mind was Joe who in most respects was just another Welsh boy. But he had begun his schooling when he was three and was a product of the slack discipline that then existed before the arrival of Mr Thomas. He was big for his age and less inhibited than most of the others so generally had a hand in any trouble that was brewing. I saw this demonstrated when I was in the infants.

The acting Head had, rather foolishly, been bestowing his favours on one of the oldest and certainly the best looking of the girls. She was allowed to ring the hand-bell that summoned us to class and performed other duties that sometimes involved staying in after school hours.

Not surprisingly this had caused tongues to wag and tales to be taken home. One afternoon the Head had been having trouble with his class and when school was dismissed the older boys with Joe in the forefront staged a demonstration. We little ones stood on the road appalled yet fascinated by the derisive shouts from the yard in which the names of the Head and the girl were mentioned.

Then there was a crash and a tinkle of glass followed by a clatter of running feet. A stone having been thrown through a window the boys came out of the yard and down the hill looking rather shocked at their temerity but still chattering and waiting on events.

The tall figure of the Head soon appeared in the girls' yard and walked down the steps into the road. In his right hand he held, vertically like a staff, the seven foot pole used for opening the top windows. He stopped a few yards from the group of boys with Joe in the front. Though shocked I remember being struck by the comic aspect of the scene. Surely, I thought, he's not going to hit anyone with that pole.

The boys were now silent and looking rather abashed. The Head asked them quietly why they had not gone home, not mentioning what they had done. Receiving no answer he said; "Now go." And they went.

I think now Mr Thomas handled Joe wisely although at the time we small fry thought he favoured him. I moved into the top class a few months before Joe left school and noticed the praise he received.

Joe was very knowledgeable about nature and knew all the calls of birds.

"What bird was that?" the Head would break off to ask when we were having a lesson outside as happened on a fine day. Hands would go up. But it was Joe who was generally asked and he always gave the right answer.

"There, you see, Joe uses his eyes and ears. That's the way to learn about Nature," the Head would say addressing the class in general.

The games we played came round in turn as mysteriously as the seasons. Once when whips and tops were in the older boys wanted to play football and told us to clear off with our tops. All except a boy named William John did. He took his top to the middle of the yard, spun it and began to whip.

Joe told him to stop. W J went on. Joe snatched the whip, broke the handle in two and flung it over the wall into the field. White faced, W J turned and marched into school to tell the Head.

We waited expectantly. After a few minutes W J came out still looking pale and joined us smaller boys.

"He isn't going to do anything," he said.

We felt badly let down. Even Wynn had to admit he could not understand why his father had decided to take no action against Joe. This, however, was not the end of the affair.

A few days later several of the bigger boys, including Joe, perhaps taking the Head's inaction as a sign of weakness, arrived late after the dinner break. They were caned. And like the others, Joe emerged from the cloakroom with his face twisted in pain and his hands pressed under his arms.

It was one of the few occasions when the Head used the cane. He caned as a punishment not as a warning for he had no need to draw the guide lines. We knew them well enough as all boys do under a firm disciplinarian. He caned in the cloakroom from whence the swish and the gasp or cry had a far greater effect on those sitting in the silence of the class room than would a 'public execution'.

Strange how one particular scene out of so many stays in the mind's eye over the years. This was an idyllic one. The steeply sloping field outside the boys' yard was used for grazing only and the farmer did not object to our going on to it occasionally. One glorious June day, when the field was white with daisies, all the girls and infants had seated themselves in little groups on the grass and were making daisy chains.

Perhaps it was a rare moment when the atmosphere acts on the mind to induce contentment. But I know that even the boys were affected by it. We called each other's attention to what the girls were doing. Some of us even went and joined them with none of the rough interplay between the sexes that was normally thought to be called for.

I saw Mr T's head appear at the window. It was 1.30 and time for the bell. But it did not ring. When finally it did the clock had moved on to 1.50. We went in in penny numbers, no lines, no spoken orders. Such leniency was unprecedented.

11

In the War years the car was a curiousity to make us stop and stare. On all but the tarred road from Beaumaris to Llangoed its approach was heralded by the loud throbbing of the engine and in dry weather by a cloud of dust.

In summer the dust made the eyes sore and covered the roadside hedges. After rain we were liable to be splashed with muddy water as the wheels bumped and swished through the brimming puddles and cart tracks. After one drenching the driver turned in his seat and laughed his silly head off.

Far more familiar was the clop of horses' hooves and the grinding rattle of iron-rimmed cart wheels. Occasionally a trotting pony would pass, proudly drawing a trap in uncanny silence with the new-fangled solid rubber wheels.

The presence of animals was pervasive. Cows, horses, sheep and sometimes pigs populated the fields. In flocks and herds they filled the narrow lanes that were widened at intervals on one side for a vehicle to draw in to let them pass. Their scents filled the air and our noses conveyed messages to the brain as they are no longer required to do in the modern sanitized world.

Farmers generally kept their stock under control. But sometimes a horse or cow would stray on to the road. I remember a horse come galloping down the narrow lane from the Camp and on to the hard surface of the Beaumaris road, its mane flying, nostrils flared and eyes glaring wildly. Trying to take the turn the rapid beat of its hooves stutter-ed as it tried to keep its balance. It slipped and fell sicken-ingly on to its side. Yet apparently unhurt it was picking itself up when a soldier appeared breathless from running. He managed to seize the bridle and calm the animal down then lead it away.

The baker's van called daily. A jovial man, he used to leave his horse contentedly cropping the grass at the side of the road as he exchanged pleasantries with Mother. On Saturday evening the butcher came with the Sunday joint. I remember him as rather morose with the barest salutation and no pleasantries.

Our coal was delivered in a farm cart. How it was ordered I am uncertain but probably an agent called at all the houses in the district. On the appointed day a collier would sail into the Straits, strand itself at hightide on the sandy beach at Friars and sit there waiting for the water to recede. Meanwhile every available farm cart for miles around would converge on the beach.

At a signal they began to trundle down the shingles to queue up in a frantic race against time as the coal was tipped into each in turn. The horses in tandem strained every muscle and sinew to haul their load up the steep shingle on to a cast iron weighing machine beside a brick hut where the clerk sat to record the weight and issue the tally. From then on the way was usually smooth. But not always.

I once saw things go badly wrong. As a cart was drawing away, the leading horse, a young and inexperienced mare, was startled and kicked violently over the traces. The close understanding between man and animal was suddenly broken. Shouting loudly the driver tugged viciously at the mare's bit and beat her into submission. She stood there oddly askew, her leg over the traces, trembling with fear and urinating like a frightened child.

The load was a ton and usually cost about a pound. We had ours tipped into a convenient angle of the wall outside the front gate. From there it had to be carried to the coal-shed in a wheel-barrow. I used to like this part as I was allowed to help with my little barrow made of a wooden box with a pram wheel. Loading up the slack with a wooden spade, I dumped it in a compartment set aside for that purpose.

Early one bright sunny morning in June, through a mist of sleep, I heard a whirring sound. They were cutting the hay in the Vicarage field. As the sound reached a crescendo I jumped out of bed and pushed back the curtains to catch sight of two horses yoked to the mower's shaft and then the mower with the man on his iron seat. They passed behind the hedge just three yards from my bedroom window.

In the soft brightness of the morning I watched the machine sweep round the borders of the field as the upright grass fell neatly into swathes in its wake. Back then to bed, but not to sleep. Instead to live in a world of sound. The whirr and clatter of the knives, slowly dying away as the mower receded in the distance; then its volume gradually rising again until it filled the room.

At seven Mother called and my day began in earnest. I looked out again. Already three swathes of grass were laid in an ever widening belt round the edge of the field. The noise of the machine as it passed the window was becoming less strident, its path moving fractionally nearer the centre at each round.

I suppose it was only imagination but the farmer who cut the hay for the Vicar had a perfect foreknowledge of the weather. Not a spot of rain held up the cutting. The mechanical horse-drawn rake would arrive in time to gather up the swathes. Moving almost at a trot, back and forth in straight lines from one side of the field to the other it would go. Its great sickle shaped prongs would fill with hay until, at the precise moment the man on his iron seat would pull the lever. Up went the prongs and down fell the hay into its place in the windrow.

That was the last of the mechanical aids. When sun and wind had done their work drying the hay, the time had come for all available hands to build the tall haycocks ready for loading on to the farm cart. The men and the Vicar himself, his face as beaming as the setting sun, went at it with their pitchforks and large wooden rakes. Even the hands of small children were at least tolerated. How we scurried excitedly throwing our contributions on the heaps until we dropped with exhaustion on to the warm scented hay, leaving the men to work steadily on.

The moment we looked forward to most was the arrival of the cart to carry the hay to be stacked at the back of the Vicarage. Alas, only once can I remember our wish granted. Every other time we came from school to find a bare stubbly field. But on that glorious evening, the Vicar with another man were still there pitching the hay up to the driver standing on top of his ever mounting load. He caught each bundle of hay and cleverly placed it in layers until at last he was standing knee deep on his mobile little haystack.

After tea Winnie and I could see that the last of the haycocks was disappearing and rushed out to beg for a ride. To our joy we were lifted up to the driver with warnings to lie flat for fear of falling or being swept off by an overhanging tree branch.

The driver slid down and went to the horse's head as we nestled in the hay, hardly daring to peep down from that dizzy height. The driver made clicking sounds out of the side of his mouth and the horse began to take the strain. We were moving, the wheels strangely silent over the stubble, the only sounds the muffled snorting of the horse and the creak of the harness.

A sudden jerk as the wheels crossed the shallow gutter between the field and the road, then the brief clatter of iron on stone and an exhilarating catch of the breath when the load swayed outwards on the sharp turn into the Vicarage drive. We crouched low now, listening to the steady thud of the horse's hooves and the crunch of the wheels on the gravel as the outstretched branches of the oak trees skimmed wisps of hay from close above us.

We were lifted down by the strong arms of the driver and stayed awhile to watch the making of the haystack. But after the ride all that was anticlimax.

Before the end of the War Father still believed the petrol engine would never replace the horse. So naturally I thought I ought to get to know the animal that would play such an important part in my life. Well, at least I tried.

Early one afternoon in the 1919 Autumn holidays I was kicking an old tennis ball against the wall outside the house, when I heard the sound of a horse approaching. It was a farmer leading a white pony. I knew him by sight and heard him referred to as Tom. A powerfully built man with square broad shoulders and spade-like hands, he was a batchelor living with his two sisters on a nearby farm.

When he came up I asked him where he was going. He stopped and said to the smithy at Beaumaris to have the pony shod. I had never been warned against talking to men I did not know, only to avoid tramps and gypsies of whom I had an irrational fear like most children. In any case I doubt if any warnings would have deterred me now. All my attention was on that beautiful white pony. It was a large one and I'd often seen it drawing the dog-cart used by Tom and his sisters.

"Please can I come for a ride?" I begged.

"O yes," Tom said. "Come on, Arthur."

He did not smile but his face had that placid, amiable look of men who work on the land and his voice was kindly. I was pleased too that he knew my name. He lifted me like a feather on to the pony's back. It had no saddle or reins but its back was comfortingly warm. I sat clinging to its mane, luxuriating in the gentle swaying motion and the sound of the steady clip, clop of its hooves. On that two mile journey I was a knight on a white horse.

Arrived at the smithy Tom lifted me down and started to
91

chat with the smith while he worked. As for me I watched fascinated. I'd never seen a horse shod. A farm horse stood docile while the smith lifted its fore leg between his knees and began paring the hoof. Didn't it hurt? Apparently not. The horse made no movement.

Then the smith went to his little furnace, held the shoe in his tongs and shuffled it in the red hot coals. He turned a little handle at the side, the sparks began to fly, the coals glowed brighter and brighter, changing to pale yellow, almost white.

Everything was done so methodically yet leisurely. At one point the smith, Tom and the other farmer turned their attention to a cannon ball in a corner of the smithy yard. It must have been six inches across. Everyone who came , apparently, had a go at lifting it with one hand, gripping it at the top. I felt sure Tom with his huge hand could do it. But both he and the farmer tried and failed.

The smith lifted it with his left hand with apparent ease. Left hand? It was years later before I found it had to be the left and not the right where the smith was concerned.

It must have been nearly two hours before Tom's turn came and the pony was shod. I was feeling tired but still elated and riding back I could hardly wait to tell Mother all the exciting things I'd seen.

I rushed in and to my surprise Mother was looking angry.

"Where have you been, you naughty boy, You've been away nearly four hours. Your Father's been and had his tea. The breadman told me he saw you riding a horse. What have you been doing?"

It was rare for Mother to go on like that, so she must have been worried. I was struck with remorse. The joy of the adventure had all but evaporated. I told her haltingly what had happened.

"If only you'd asked me," Mother said, "You must never do a thing like that again. You had me worried sick."

I promised. The knight on a white horse was unseated. Life went on its humdrum way. The only bright spot was I'd got to know a little about man's best friend.

In Spring the following year I had the chance to increase my knowledge. William Jones, the carter at Bryn Hyfryd was one of nature's gentlemen. He was of medium height and sturdily built. In most weathers he wore a waistcoat over his rough grey shirt and his corduroy trousers were tied with string below the knee in the traditional manner of all farm workers as a precaution against rats or mice running up their

legs. Beneath the cap that covered his balding head his wrinkled walnut face would break into a smile when he saw
Winnie (he called her Queenie), or me for he was never too
busy to greet even a small child.

This Spring day in 1920 he let me accompany him with
Drummer and Jessie. the black shire horses, to the Army
Camp, now in the last stages of demolition. He swung me
on to Drummer's back and walked between the pair, leading
them by their bridles. I seemed to be an immense height,
much higher than on the white pony. I clung to the horns of
the collar, my legs spread almost horizontally across the
broad back. We moved off and as Drummer got into his
stride the ground began to revolve past when I looked down.

I'd been looking forward to seeing the place where all the
soldiers had lived and trained for the War. It was a great
disappointment. The huts I'd remembered seeing from the
road when they were vibrant with life had all gone. Only a
few buildings and the concrete foundations with heaps of
poles and planks of wood were left. It was like a graveyard.

William became engrossed in conversation with one of the
soldiers still on the site while I sat and looked around. The
horses were at last brought into use, dragging timber from
different parts of the camp to be stacked up.

We were home for dinner at 12 and I told Mother that Mr
Jones had said I could go with him in the afternoon. At 1pm
prompt I waited for him outside the cottage in which the
workers had their meal. We crossed the road to where the
horses were waiting at the gate. Taking Jessie by the face
harness William led her up the field to the stables. To give
me something to do, I suppose, he said:

"Round up Drummer, Arthur."

Drummer was already following anyway. But I began
shouting the encouraging "Gee-ups" I'd heard the farmers
use. We were half way across the field with Drummer about
six yards ahead of me. What happened next I can see as
clearly as though I have just watched a re-run on film.

Without any warning, Drummer wheeled sharply to his left
and broke into a gallop straight at where I was standing. I
can still hear the sound of his thudding hooves and, as in a
camera still, see the frontal view of the great black horse,
all its feet off the ground, its fore legs curved back as it
charged.

Petrified, I raised my left arm to cover my face and felt
the wind of the huge shape as it hurtled past, missing me by
inches. Seconds later I turned round fearfully. Drummer had
stopped 50 yards away and turned to face me. He raised his

head, snorted, shook his head and started quietly to crop the grass.

William by now had almost reached the stable with Jessie. I walked slowly in his direction. He had not seen what happened and I said that Drummer had run away and I couldn't stop him. William just smiled his wrinkled smile then walked down to where Drummer was eating and led him back like a lamb.

Seated again on Drummer's broad back I felt none of the morning's elation. In my mind there lurked a devil in that enormous frame below me ready to leap out. I spent the afternoon in the Camp and returned on Drummer's back.

It was my last attempt to come to terms with 'man's best friend'. I told no one of my shock and fears. They would not understand. Only girls were afraid. Boys had to be brave at all times.

I think now that Drummer was just having a bit of fun at my expense and had no intention of harming me. Assuming of course that horses have a sense of humour

I still thought they were beautiful to look at. They were at their best in the autumn as they strode majestically before the plough. In the hazy sunlight the muffled beat of hooves, the nodding heads, the clank of chains and the hiss of the ploughshare as it peeled aside the brown earth, with the ploughman guiding both horse and plough, was a sight to treasure in the mind's eye.

The scene was beloved of artists in children's books. I used to copy these pictures and must have become quite good at it. One of my sketches so impressed a boy in my class that he asked me to lend it to him to enter a competition at an eisteddfod at Llangoed Village Hall. I declined and asked him if I could enter it myself. He bore no resentment and told me what I had to do.

I was about ten at the time and had been a few times to the Hall. The first was immediately after the War when Father took us to see 'moving pictures' brought there by a travelling showman. The projector was hand operated and the pictures that appeared on the canvas screen flickered and sparked for a few minutes at a time between breakdowns. We thought it was wonderful.

By this time I had got to know some of the Llangoed boys by name. Perhaps because they were a more closely knit community they seemed more clannish that we were at Penmon. The Hall was packed and we sat at the back, all dolled up in our Sunday best. None of us took much interest in the singing which was the main adult attraction. But the antics of the conductors of the competing choirs so roused our amusement that we found it hard to contain.

There were lads from other villages present and it was clear that the locals were keen to have a barney with them, so I received my first insight into the rituels of gang warfare. A group of foreigners immediately in front of us became our natural enemies. Their leader kept glaring back at us and was subjected to hissed threats as to what would happen to him unless he minded his own business.

During the interval one of them went out to the toilet. As he came back the boy at the end of our row left his foot dangling invitingly in the aisle. The foreigner obliged by kicking it out of the way and stopped to try and outstare the row of angry faces thrust forward in his direction.

"Punch him, Will." hissed our leader.

However, Will was not disposed to go out on a limb that far and his assailant strutted back to his seat, honour vindicated.

I won first prize for the ploughing scene.

Although contrary to Father's prediction the horse was soon to disappear from the roads and fields, another of man's best friends is still very much with us. And then as now it was our desire as children to have one of our own. And we did.

He was Mickey, a black and white mongrel terrier that Tillis bought for Winnie in 1920. For two eventful years he was a member of the family and our constant companion.

Like all pups he was engaging and soon learnt to sit up and beg for food. He also had an insatiable urge to fetch anything thrown for him. For this there were no shortage of helpers. One twelve year old girl we were friendly with flung a stone about 45 degrees off target and caught me smack between the eyes. The wound bled profusely and I still have the scar.

Mickey had an unusual characteristic. He seemed to lack the pack instinct and failed to accord the most common courtesies to other dogs. At their appearance his immediate reaction was to attack. I have never known a dog so aggressive and fearless. He had many scraps that usually ended with honours even.

That is until one Sunday afternoon when he was a year and a half old when he sighted an Airedale out for a walk with its owner. Mickey pricked up his ears, set up his back

95

hair, gathered his strength and flew. The contest could hardly have been more one-sided. In seconds the Airedale had Mickey by the hind leg and was shaking him like a rat.

With great difficulty the two were separated. Inspection showed that apart from sundry gashes, the top of Mickey's hind leg was almost bitten through. Two weeks convalescence were needed before he could run about again.

Not long afterwards the Airedale reappeared, this time on a lead. Without hesitation, Mickey flew again to the attack. The Airedale's owner had to fight him off with a stick he now prudently carried, before he could be dragged away yelping and snarling defiance.

In the summer of 1922 Mickey took to disappearing in the afternoon and would not be seen again until the evening. His whereabouts in these intervals remained a mystery for several weeks. Then one evening a boy arrived on a bicycle leading him, very subdued and bedraggled on a piece of string. He had fallen off the Cynfal just as it had reached the landing stage at Beaumaris, the boy said. The tide was flowing and he would have been swept away had not one of the crew dived in and rescued him. We showered the little dog with affection but he seemed strangely unresponsive.

How did he come to be on the ferry, we wondered. He had fallen off as it was landing so, incredible as it seemed, he must have been to Bangor. In the days that followed we managed to piece together a remarkable story.

Tillis had taken Mickey with him to Bangor several times, catching the bus outside the house, getting off at Beaumaris walking down the pier, sailing to Bangor on the Cynfal, walking into the City and having tea in Robert Roberts' restaurant in the main street. There Mickey had entertained the customers by begging at the tables.

Evidence now emerged that, over a year later, he had been making the same journey on his own, attaching himself to different passengers on the bus and ferry and begging in the restaurant.

Father sought out his rescuer and gave him half a crown, apologising for the smallness of the reward for his heroism. But a change had come over Mickey. It seems likely that he received a knock on the head when he fell. Whatever the reason, he was no longer his lively self and at unexpected moments would turn the aggression he had previously shown against his own kind upon the human race.

He snapped at several people for no reason. He even snapped at me when I was stroking him, drawing a trickle of blood. Then one afternoon my cousin Bert on holiday from Bootle told us he had seen Mickey on Beaumaris pier with group of youngsters who were baiting him while he darted at them snarling. Older people shook their heads.

"That dog's a menace. He should be put down before he hurts somebody."

I think Father had already decided what to do. But Mickey came home and put the matter beyond doubt by biting Winnie. He was tied up outside and we were told not to go near him. The poor little wretch seemed to know. He did not attempt to get away; just lay there looking woebegone.

Next day Father made the arrangements. After work he led Mickey off across the fields to a man with a shot gun who had promised to do what was necessary for a small fee.

Father came home alone. He did not say what happened but I knew for I'd seen another dog put down. Its brains were shot out at point blank range.

Poor Mickey. It was all so long ago and you were only a mongrel. So why on earth I should still feel sad for you goodness knows. Perhaps it was your spirit and acceptance of your fate that could teach us humans a thing or two.

From the age of eight, trespassing became an exciting game and from it developed my love of nature. It began with the strip of woods to the Vicarage. But soon the densely wooded estate of Tre Castell on the other side of the road became my hunting ground. Among the many nests I found at Tre Castell was a pheasant's on the ground with thirteen eggs in it. I took one for my collection, blowing out the contents through a pin hole in the narrow end and out of a slightly bigger one at the other; then I put it in the box lined with cotton wool with the rest.

The gardener at Tre Castell, was a friend of Father's. He used to come along on a fine evening for a chin-wag. Not that there was much talking from him. He just sat there radiating contentment through a haze of pipe smoke, his brown face wrinkled into a faint smile round the eyes.

On one visit he mentioned the trouble he had been having with bullfinches in the orchard, getting at the fruit buds and said he would have to trap them. I had watched these beautiful birds and knew their call. But what had really fixed them in my mind was seeing them outside the lodge at Henllys near the church. Mr See, the old gardener had at least half a dozen in cages and this day he had put them outside in the sun. The cage doors were open and the birds were flying in and out. I was amazed to see how they seemed to regard the cages as their home and did not want to escape to freedom. He must have had some special skill in taming them for I have never seen the like again.

So when I heard Mr Owen say he was going to trap these bullfinches I asked him if he would give me one to keep in a cage. A few weeks later he brought one in the trap cage he had used and transferred it to a big cage we had. To find out what to do I had bought a sixpenny book on 'British Cage Birds' which gave information on what to feed each one on and how to tame them.

It said the bullfinch was one of the easiest to tame and that it needed a lot of rape, an oily seed, to keep it fit. True enough in a fortnight it was coming to the bars to take bits of apple from my fingers and giving them playful nips. He was not much of a singer but would warble away softly to itself.

Of course caging wild birds is now illegal. But then it was a part of country life and reflected the love of nature. Even now I could not fail to recognise the call of a bullfinch however faint and how it recalls my friendship with that little bird.

12

Although we lacked most modern sporting facilities, we were as mad on football as schoolboys are today. Until about two years after the War we played all our games in the yard which, like the foundations of the school, had been laid by digging into a steep slope and using the soil and rubble to raise the level at the lower end.

The top of the yard was thus bounded by an eight foot high retaining wall. Above this tall trees towered on the ascending slope to shelter us completely from the North wind. At the other end the infants' and girls' yards were raised about ten feet above the road.

The yard's surface was of clay soil rammed down hard by the feet of children scurrying over it for a quarter of a century. Old-fashioned, maybe. But admirably adapted for all our games. It was hard enough for tops to spin on; sloping enough to shed most of the rain, yet retaining enough in places to allow a thin sheet of ice to form for a slide on a frosty morning. And when the time for marbles came round, saucer shaped holes could be scraped in it for us to take aim at.

As a football pitch, however, it had its limitations. It was small and triangular. Only at the retaining wall end could a goal be made with big stones and corners taken, the exact width of the goal being a subject of frequent argument. On the width of the other goal there could be no disagreement. It was fixed naturally by the corner of the building and the wall on the road side where they funnelled to a gap no more than 8 feet wide.

These restrictions called for specialised skills in the players. Possession was nine tenth of the game. A clever dribbler would tend to keep the ball, (which was any kind we could get and usually the size of a tennis ball), until he lost it or scored a goal. He rarely condescended to pass except as a friendly gesture. The rest had to wait for the ball to come loose and try a shot at goal. With no touch lines and no throw-ins, the ricochet off the wall was a special art. It could be used to get round an opponent or to score an in-off past the goalie at the narrow end.

99

The most skilful exponent of the game was a rather small, sloping shouldered boy named Dick Pells who could slip like an eel past an opponent or emerge with the ball from a milling, kicking scrum of players up against a wall. Dick was always first choice of a captain in the pick-up that preceded the game.

Until 1920 we played happily enough in these conditions. But about this time Penmon started up a football team and as their pitch was in the field near the school we were allowed to use it once or twice a week. It had real goal posts with cross-bars painted white and lines marked by digging up narrow strips of turf and turning them earth side up. Nets and a contraption for marking the lines with white-wash were acquired later.

The field transformed out game. We had not seen profess-ionals play but we had learnt the various positions and kept to them religiously; the winger stayed on his wing, the cent-re-forward up in the middle of the field, closely shadowed by the opposing centre-half. To wander from ones territory was strictly taboo. Some dribblers were still pests, hanging on to the ball, making no progress towards the opponent's goal and keeping the rest of us waiting in our respective positions.

One exception was Dick Pells who quickly adapted his game and became our best inside forward. Another was Sam Jones, a dribbler of a different sort. Sammy had a cast in his eye and wore glasses for school work. He was thin legged and slim built but had good shoulders. He would move forward at an uncertain pace with a curious teetering run as though about to fall on his face. Yet, against all the odds, he usually came out of a tackle with the ball. He had a clever technique to counter the shoulder charge of heavier opponents. Just as the opposing player committed himself to the charge Sam would check his stride for a split second to allow his opponent to hurtle through the air and fall to the ground in a heap. He would then resume his teetering run never having lost control of the ball.

I can recall only one game we played against another school. This was a home fixture against Llangoed which had far more boys to choose from and outmatched us for size. Their captain, Emrys Owen, was particularly big, tough and aggressive. They had real football boots too while some of us had to turn out in ordinary old boots with studs hammered in.

By half-time we were 3-0 down and pretty demoralised. Mr T did make a half hearted attempt to buck us up with a few words of encouragement. But we hardly listened. Our eyes were all on our opponents. Their teacher had taken them a few yards away and was giving them each a half orange to suck. I don't know what good it did them, but by the effect it had on us he could have given them a magic elixir. Those half oranges destroyed any vestiges of confidence we had left.

As the second half proceeded our efforts became weaker and weaker. Our wretched dribblers indulged their fancy foot work for a moment when a heavy footed defender crashed in to send the ball flying to his waiting forwards. In retrospect the only member of our team to emerge with honour was the goalie. He kept out all but 10. Yet we had the nerve to blame him in a half-hearted way for our defeat.

Emrys. the Llangoed captain I later came to know quite well. He was one of the most dedicated footballers I have known. Once when some of us were getting in some practice on the Common at Llangoed, I was distracted by the antics of some small boys kicking a tennis ball about. I laughed and was pointing them out just as our ball came in my direction. I missed it and Emrys soon brought me back to the stern realities of life with a scathing:

"Yes, but it's football they're playing isn't it."

When I last saw Emrys he was 74 and as dedicated as ever coaching and encouraging the youth of Llangoed.

Llangoed had many chapels but no pubs. Drinkers had to travel to Beaumaris where there was no dearth of inns. Sammy D---- who played in the forward line for Penmon soon after the team was started used to make the trip to Town regularly. His precise condition on his return was hard to gauge for Sammy had a rolling gait at all times. He would turn up for the game on Saturday having taken on a few and would still play a blinder.

But his fame rested on his ability as a taker of penalties. For two seasons he never missed. Utterly relaxed, he would roll up to the ball and slot it right-footed never more than a foot inside the left hand post. Mesmerised by the sublime confidence of that run up the opposing goalie rarely moved before turning to retrieve the ball from the net.

But came the inevitable day. I remember it well though I was not at the match.

"Haven't you heard? Sammy has missed a penalty."

"Never!"

"He did I tell you. I was there. Saw it with my own eyes. Missed by a yard."

Sammy played on to the end of the season. He took more penalties. Scored some but missed again. The magic had gone. Just another penalty taker. Sic transit.

At one match I was puzzled by the use of a word. The start of the game was delayed because a player had not arrived. At last the captain came over and asked a young fellow if he would play. Certainly he would. He took off his Sunday best jacket and waistcoat, donned the football shirt and stepped on to the muddy field.

"Aren't you afraid he'll get himself dirty?" a bystander asked the proud mother.

"Oh, no," she said, "It's only clean dirt isn't it."

I quietly asked Father what she meant. He said, "She just means it's only dirt from the field. There aren't any cows about or anything like that, so it'll soon brush off."

In those early days when Penmon was in the early stages of team building, Father only went to see them occasionally, out of a sense of loyalty. The team he supported was St Mary's of Beaumaris. Like many a more famous side this had been started for the young men of the local church, though by now, in the interests of success, membership had become less exclusive.

After dinner on Saturday, as a small boy, I would trek along with him the two miles along the Friars road and up across the fields to the ground about half a mile outside the town. It think he used to go as much for a natter with the Beaumaris worthies and hear the latest gossip as to watch the game

One these was a retired butcher, an old man but still a formidable looking figure with wide shoulders and heavy features. His conversation invariably seemed to get round to the doings of one of his sons who was apparently doing great things in the world. Father was always ready to lend an ear to such domestic matters though I could never understand why as it seemed so one-sided and boring.

Rivalry between the opposing teams was at times intense and could take some queer turns. One of these involved the old butcher. A rival spectator kept hanging around where we were standing and staring pointedly in our direction. I could sense that his attention was focussed on the old man who was declaiming as usual in a loud voice on the virtues of his son with occasional asides on merits of the opposing team thrown in. At last this individual came up and asked the old butcher why he kept staring at him.

The old boy immediately put up his fists and told the fellow to clear off or he'd knock his head off. A group of local supporters crowded round and the man, realising he was in enemy territory took the wise course and slunk off.

St Mary's had a strong team at that time including an ex-Irish International named Joe Irons at right back. Irons had come to the district as a gentleman's valet I believe, and was a tall, slim dapper man who, in spite of his age was still more than a match for most opposing forwards.

The game that always drew the largest crowds was against nearby Llandegfan, the area between Beaumaris and Menai Bridge. They too sported an ex-International, a Welshman named named Oliver who, by a happy coincidence played on the left wing. He was tall with a slight stoop and although quite old, obvious knew a deal about playing on the wing. In the minds of many, much interest was focussed on the duel between the two old-stagers.

I remember one of these games on account of an incident at the start of the second half. The scores were even with the chief danger to the Beaumaris goal coming from the accurate centres from Oliver's runs to the goal line. He had again given the left half the slip at the centre line and was heading smoothly for the corner flag with a clear run ahead. Irons who appeared to have been having trouble with his boot was standing near his goal. He sprang to life and raced to cut off his opponent. But would he catch him? He did and in a spectacular manner shoulder charged Oliver over the touchline and over the rope holding back the spectators.

This proved the turning point in the game. From then on Llandegfan were demoralised with poor Oliver slowed down with a limp - and of course Beaumaris won. The varied opinions of opposing spectators on that shoulder charge need no elaboration.

Of the rest of the team, Frank Williams, the left back, was a University student. Strongly built with bushy black hair, he was rock-like and a foil to Irons. Frank was tragically killed in a motor cycle accident on the winding Garth road soon after he graduated. I never pass the spot by the large gated entrance to the Bulkeley estate without thinking of that early sacrifice to the combustion engine.

The right winger, Joe Hender, was of medium height, bony

and broad shouldered with a reddish nose. Happy-go-lucky Joe had a quick wit. Once when he was fouled he looked up at his opponent, grinned and came out with what was the catch phrase of the moment, "How's yer father?" From then on Joe became affectionatyely known to the fans a "How's yer father".

One Saturday he was displaced by a stranger who had arrived on the scene from Merseyside. This chap had a convincing line of talk and said he had played for Everton A. This so impressed the selectors they decided to give him a trial.

This was the age when footballers wore long baggy shorts a la Alex James the great Scottish and Arsenal forward. So there was general surprise when the stranger turned out in very short shorts. In spite of this flouting of conventions and thinking they might be witnessing a new fashion, all were ready to give him the benefit of the doubt.

But after ten minutes it became obvious that the man was either a fraud or had misjudged our standard of play. He kept failing to beat his opponent, miskicked repeatedly and even fell over for no particular reason. From then on the wits had a field day and as he was on the wing, there was no escape. I can still see one spectator, tears of laughter running down his face as he gasped, "Just look at those shorts".

The stranger never played again though he did gain from his experience. He became known as 'Everton A'. Strangely, he never seemed to mind the sarcasm. The fact of being recognised was apparently its own reward.

Other players I remember were Ellis Wyn, the left winger. Small and very fast, he was a well known sprinter at the Summer sports meetings all over the Island. Years later he lent me his running spikes when I started to compete at these meetings for much needed spare cash.

Then there were the Humphries brothers. One playing at inside left had been a professional while Walter, the youngest was a strong centre-half. The other inside forward was Charlie Connolly, a contemporary of my eldest brother at the Grammar School.

Only once do I remember St Mary's crossing the Straits for a match. They had been issued an invitation or challenge, by a team which I think was called Llechid Celts. Father went to support and came back with a lurid account of what happened.

The ground was on a mountain side and the club had had great difficulty in constructing a pitch of adequate size. On one side was the mountain while the other had a touch-line marked by a drystone wall beyond which was a steep slope with officials posted to retrieve any ball that came over. To suit this unusual pitch the home side had amended some of the rules of which they had conveniently omitted to inform the visitors before the game started.

When the ball was struck against the wall, our side stopped, expecting a throw in. Not so the Celts who pressed on and scored. The referee then explained that only when the ball went over the wall would there be a throw in. That was the rule and the goal would have to stand.

St Mary's were unable to adapt to this departure from the norm, particularly as their opponents were, like the lads at my school, adept at using the in-off the wall technique to pass an opponent. This and the ref, who according to Father "knew whose side he was on" gave them no chance and they were heavily defeated.

I believe the mountain men remained content with their victory and did not venture a return match on the flat lands of Beaumaris.

13

My brother Jack hated school and left a year early to work on Tre Castell farm for a few shillings a week. A contempory of his told me recently of an incident that may have brought this about. The two waited after school for the head mistress to go to the earth closet, then waggled some furze under her bottom from the back. Next morning she accused them in private but on advice from the curate not to make a fuss she told the parents to take them away. All this fits in with my early recollection of my feeling upset by Jack being taken outside by Father and walloped with a stick.

His fixed ambition was to be a sailor when old enough. So at 14 he was packed off to join a merchant ship in London as cabin boy. The venture lasted less than 24 hours. Nobody told me why at the time and Jack only years later. The skipper made crude sexual advances so he walked off the ship and came home.

It was back to the farm and an uneasy peace between him and Father. Then one evening at harvest time the farmer brought Jack home with a blood-stained bandage over most of his face. His nose had been pierced to the bone by a pitchfork. My parents decided that was enough of farming. As soon as the wound had healed over Jack began work as an under gardener at Penrhyn Castle on the other side of the Straits.

Partly no doubt because he had no desire to follow in his father's footsteps, Jack liked gardening no more than school. Reports leaked out that he was slacking. One asserted that he was spending too much time in the WC. Jack told me later this was true. He was fed up with digging, weeding and pot washing under a domineering overseer. Sitting in the WC or pretending to was the best way of getting away from it all for a break.

He was the most generous of my brothers and took the trouble of bringing me the prize exhibit of my collection of birds' eggs; a heron's, whose large, white oval shape eclipsed even the green and brown speckled sea-gull's that someone had given me after a trip to Puffin Island.

One day when he had the day off he took Winnie and me

to school. He asked me if anyone was bullying me and if so he would have great pleasure in sorting him out. I said 'No'. Not quite true of course. But I had the feeling that any interference by Jack would make matters worse after he'd gone. He took us via Llangoed and gave us four pence each. This was four times my weekly allowance and I wanted to save half. But no. He insisted it was all spent.

So we called in at the sweet shop at the bottom of Mona Terrace and went to school with pockets stuffed with sweets, liquourice sticks and chewing gum. Alas, as with all such joyful occasions the worm was in the bud. I'd never had chewing gum before and knowing no better, chewed and swallowed the lot. From mid-day on it lay like lead on my stomach. I had a miserable night and went to school feeling below par. I still have an aversion to the stuff.

For my tenth birthday Jack bought me the finest birthday present I've ever had - a real size four leather football. It must have cost him a packet. That was May 1922 and all the family went for a picnic down past Tre Castell farm to the beach where there was a stretch of grass. Ernie was there, so with Jack, myself and a few passers by we had a good kick around.

Jack had to leave at 6 and walk along the cliffs to Friars road to catch the bus to Bangor. Just before it was time for him to go he mis-kicked the ball hard and high into the thicket of trees and bushes between the beach and the farm field. The growth was so dense we found it impossible to get in to look for it. I was upset but Jack even more. Time was getting short and he had to go. But before leaving he insisted I take two half crowns to make up for the loss.

Fortunately we managed to retrieve the ball soon after he had gone, and he got his half crowns back when he came home a week later.

Having had the sailor bug driven out of his system Jack could hardly wait until he was 18 to join the Army. In the early Autumn of that year he enlisted in the REs. About a year later he was posted to Bere Island in Bantry Bay, then part of the South Ireland Coast Defences. (Coincidentally I was posted to Spike Island in Cork Harbour 12 years later).

Of the two Bere Island was the most isolated and to pass the time Jack began to construct wireless sets - a misnomer if ever there was one for, these early radio receivers were criss-crossed with a maze of wires connecting the valves, condensers, coils etc. Nearly all his leaves were spent in building ever more elaborate sets. As soon as a meal was over the table cloth was removed and on the kitchen table would go the set's components, the soldering iron, the solder and fluxite. No electricity or gas so the iron had to be heated in the fire. So wrapt was he in the work that hardly a word could be had out of him all day.

He never got a set to work quite to his satisfaction. The BBC would come through and we would each have a listen. Then he would decide that some modification was needed which meant several days frustration with no listening. But when the end of his leave came he left a set in working order and Father began the rituel he kept up the rest of his life, tuning in to the six and nine o'clock news bulletins.

Reception was by an aerial more than 100 feet long, slung as high as possible between two oak trees, one in the Vicarage woods, the other in the far corner of the garden. Soon came the first 'loudspeaker' and we could all listen together.

What do I remember? First I think was the euphony of words the like of which I had never heard. Even the shipping forecasts with Rockald, Mallin and Shannon sounded like poetry to my ears. On Saturday came the Football Results, and here it was Scottish and Irish names I loved to hear. What romance there was in names of which I knew nothing but the sounds - Heart of Midlothian, Motherwell, Queen of the South, Partick Thistle, Coleraine and Glentoran.

Before the end of his tour on Bere Island Jack was given a small bunk where he could pursue his hobby. And the Commanding Officer used to call in and listen. Not bad for a school 'drop out'!

After a time in London, working with his hands was losing its attraction for Ernie. His active mind was turning to more intellectual and artistic channels. In 1918 he was drafted into the Royal Artillery. He boxed as a welter-weight and, prickly as ever once had an NCO before the CO for swearing at him. His last manual job was porter at the Grosvenor Hotel, Chester. His grandmother, (Mary Tilston), now in her 80s, was also living in the City with her daughter Annie. Edith was there too, working as a seamstress at Brown's and lodging at the YWCA. for a while.

Early in 1922 he came home on the dole and spent much of his time making pencil sketches out of doors and indoors in pen and ink. He sold a few to the gentry including two of Llanfaes Church at £5 each. Another one was framed and hung in our house until Father died. A few year ago I had it renovated. The draughtsmanship is so fine that the expert thought it the work of a professional.

In the 1923 General Election he upset Father by actively supporting the Labour Candidate. Knowing it would be useless to say anything, Father had to hold his horses. Sometime in 1924 Ernie left for Liverpool as an agent in the Pearl Assurance Company. From then on he was financially secure.

THE FIRST
FENCE

14

For most of my life the memory of my eldest brother has lain dormant in the recesses of my mind. Exactly why I cannot say. It may have been the desire felt by the young to forget the War as a bad dream. Or perhaps it was because Winnie and I were deliberately shielded at the time from a realisation of what was happening to him.

When the War broke out he was 20 and was taking a science degree at Bangor University. He volunteered but was turned down apparently because his chest measurements did not match his height which was 5ft 11ins. He returned to his studies and at the end of the Easter Term was awarded a bursary.

Early in May 1915 he tried again to enlist and either the regulations had been relaxed or his chest had developed for he was accepted by the Royal Welch Fusileers. Before completing his training he volunteered for the newly formed gas section of the Royal Engineers and a few weeks later was in France as a corporal taking part in the first British gas attack at the Battle of Loos.

He had been recommended for a commission and in October returned to Tenby on an officers' training course in the Welsh Regiment. In the Spring of 1916 he was returned to France as a 2nd lieutenant where, after nine months on the Somme he went down with trench fever. The cause of the desease remained a mystery throughout the War. Even when it was finally traced to a parasite in the excreta of fleas, often blown about as a fine dust that entered the blood stream through a cut, no antedote was discovered.

Symptoms included high temperature and severe rheumatic pains accompanied by sensitivity of the skin so acute that even the pressure of bedclothes became unbearable. The desease was likely to recur and certainly Tillis never fully recovered. He was invalided home and after a brief convalescence was declared unfit for active service and then posted to Training Camps. first at Yarmouth then Kinmel Park in North Wales. He was demobbed on Christmas Day 1918 with the rank of captain.

For a short while I saw quite a lot of him. He had bought

a motor bike and sidecar and although he used to take Mother out most, Winnie and I had a few rides on this exhilarating new means of transport. He also promised that when the sun got stronger he would take me for my first dip in the sea. He must have found it hard to fit in because the time was soon after 7 on a morning in early June.

I still remember the thrill of excitement on the way to Friars beach sitting on the pillion seat of the bike and clinging to the thick leather belt he had on. Then the shock of immersion and the tang of that first gulp of salt sea water. It was a most unpleasant experience yet I managed to delude myself it was thoroughly enjoyable.

After the first Summer I saw far less of Tillis and supposed that most of his time was taken up with studying for his degree. Long afterwards Mother said he had found it hard after his war experiences and recurrence of Trench Fever. He was awarded his BSc in 1920 after a shortened course for ex-servicemen and obtained a post as science master at Caernarvon County School.

Although he came home at weekends he had little to do with me from now on. He spent a lot of time with Mother and at times were exchanging confidences on some matter of deep concern. He took her about a good deal in the sidecar. Indeed I believe she did more travelling at this time than at any other in her life.

Winnie and I would ask if we could be taken out too. But Mother always made some excuse. At last we accepted the fact and sought other activities.

I had noticed that for some time Tillis had a bandage round his neck. Then, quite suddenly, soon after Easter 1921, we were told he had given up the teaching post and was in a sanatorium for TB in Caernarvon.

I have a vague memory of being taken to see him. The place was close to the mountains and seemed cold even in summer. It had white painted woodwork, large glass windows thrown open, with long verandahs on to which the beds could be pulled. For clean fresh air was regarded as an essential part of the treatment, even when in a feverish heat the patients were having their clothing changed.

He spoke to us quite cheerfully but the bandage was still round his neck and I could see another wrapped round his chest.

He remained in the sanatorium all that summer and though I was not informed, it was clear from overheard conversation that he was getting no better. Then at the end of August we were told he was coming home. On the medical evidence nothing more could be done for him so my parents decided he must be with us for his last days. Mother would nurse him under the directions of the local doctor and Edith would give up her job to help run the home.

Obviously he could not be accommodated in the house so a small wooden chalet was ordered. This had to travel in sections to Bangor by train and brought the last 8 miles on a horse drawn cart. Miss Pritchard, hearing that Tillis had paid his consultant's fees himself and had refused to apply for a pension, offered Father any financial help that was needed. Mother, her pride still hurt at Miss P's coolness on hearing that Tillis had been commissioned, sent her thanks and said "We can manage."

There was anxiety as to whether the chalet would arrive on time and whether it would stand too high in the cart to pass under the arches of Menai Bridge, (which have since been raised to take modern vehicles). The problem was solved by unloading the sections at each arch and re-loading on the other side.

I caught a fleeting sight of Tillis when he was brought in but only once after that. We were enjoined to be quiet about the house and encouraged to go out as much as possible. I did not see much of Mother and the strain on Father came out in his irritability. Once when he was 'going off the deep end' about something, Tillis could hear him. He only smiled and said, "Just like old times." Mother told me that years later.

Edith remembered a remark that seems comic now in spite of the circumstancs. Once after Father had been in to talk to him, Tillis said to her: "I do wish he wouldn't keep his hat on when he sits here." In mitigation I should add that Father was going bald and was no doubt feeling the cold in the chalet with the windows open.

In the second week of November Mother's great friend Mrs Bloss left her family to fend for themselves and came to take turns in the round the clock attendance that was now needed. Then one evening in the third week Mother told Winnie and me that Tillis was very ill and wanted to see us.

We went in feeling subdued like going into church. His head was propped up on pillows and he looked pale though his eyes were bright. He asked how we were getting on at school. Then he told us to work hard and be good to Mother and do as she said. Mother had told us we could kiss him on the cheek. When we had done this we went out.

112

That was the last I saw of him. He died in the early hours of November 21st. I believe he kept his Christian faith and had been resigned and uncomplaining to the end. We had been so prepared for his death that I felt no overwhelming grief. Besides I had had so little to do with him for more than a year.

But now I have thought of how he survived the Great War and was granted three years grace only to be gathered in like a straggler from that lost generation. I have also found out why he had so little to say to Winnie and me towards the end. After the TB was confirmed he had deliberately avoided close contact with us younger ones for fear of passing on the desease which was then incurable.

A few days before he died Winnie and I had been taken in by our near neighbours, the Monks, at Rhos Cottage. Effie, the 16 year old daughter who did most of the housework for her parents, took charge of us. Dear Effie. How I remember her cheerful kindness, keeping us company when we came home from school and reading to us from the Christmas Annual before bed time. I'm sure we were ungrateful at the time and never expressed our thanks. Not that that would have made any difference to Effie. It was her nature to give cheerfully.

We were excluded from the funeral and did not go home until it was over. But on the day we did not go to school. I thought the cortege would pass Rhos Cottage on its way to church and kept going to the gate to see if it was coming. Once when I was looking out I was surprised to see a boy I knew walking past. It was Joe Roberts. He stopped and asked why I wasn't at school. When I told him he said in tones I'd never heard him use before how sorry he was about Tillis. Then he said that he'd left school and was on his way to start work on a farm. Mr T had let him leave three months before he was 14.

After seeing this new side of Joe I felt differently towards him. But with the news of his leaving a niggling uncertainty was lifted. From then on life would be more predictable. I never saw Joe again.

I continued to look out for the cortege but in vain. It had gone the longer but better road past Friars beach.

We went home the next day and life seemingly resumed its old routine. But things were not really the same. There were times when Mother could not hide her grief and that only made Father more irritable, no doubt from a feeling of helplessness.

The following Easter Mother had taken to her bed for the first time I had known. Exactly why I was not told though later I learnt it was shingles. Edith had again taken over so on a bright but cold Easter Sunday morning we went off to church as usual leaving her to do the cooking.

For Christians the day is said to be the most joyful in the Calendar. But for me that Easter Sunday morning stands as one of the most miserable of my life. I was old enough now to comprehend the words of the Service. They told us that Christ had risen. At the same time they harped on the theme of his dying and how we must all die.

Jesus lives; henceforth is death
But the gate of life immortal;
This shall calm our trembling breath
When we pass its gloomy portal.
Alleluia.

The message came all too clear. We were all going to die and the sooner we got it over with the better. 'Life immortal' sounded grand but it did not seem to mean much to me. I couldn't help seeing God as a reflection of everyone I knew in authority. Most of them took a pretty poor view of my failings. And God saw EVERYTHING. I knew the part about 'suffer little children'. But I had a feeling that only applied to Sundays. The rest of the week it would be back to 'children should be seen and not heard'.

We walked home with Father as usual and were greeted with the same appetising odour of roast beef and potatoes. But a vital spark was missing. Edith took us into the bedroom to see Mother. We stood beside the sick bed just as we had done at Tillis' a few months before. Mother was pale and did not raise her head. She spoke quietly in a voice drained of emotion. I felt tongue-tied with that terrible tightness in the throat. Then we filed out to dinner.

Such moods of dark depression rarely last for long when you are young and from then on I began to perk up. Dinner tasted as good as usual and the rest of the day passed with no more solemnity and gloom than any other Sunday.

Mother was soon back on her feet and into her daily routine. Selfishly I assumed she was well again. She was not. Yet so rigid was the rule of 'not in front of the children' I was not told of or suspected the angina pectoris which was diagnosed by a consultant not long after.

"You have been a very healthy woman, Mrs Haley," he said "but that is no longer so and you will have to take things easy."

Good advice. But the puritan ethic was too engrained. Her pretty lips untouched by any cosmetic became a little firmer. Her hands were never idle. Years later a daughter-in-law with the self-assurance of a liberated woman commented:

"Thank heaven, with modern gadgets I'll never have to slave like your mother."

How little she understood. Mother was sustained by a religious faith of the purest simplicity; seeing 'the Gates of Heaven' in a golden sunset; believing that good would always triumph over evil in the end.

Once when I was troubled she put her arm round me and said: "Don't worry, Everything will come right in the end. I know Tillis will send angels to keep watch over you."

I was just in my teens and so struck with surprise at the idea my troubles evaporated for the moment. Cold reason had by then destroyed any hope of such supernatural help. An intellectual gulf had already open up between her and me. Yet now I know that in the end the heart transcends cold reason. And who can tell which is right.

Beaumaris Grammar School

INSCRIPTION ON MEMORIAL TABLET

Praise God for the service of these Bimarensians
who, amid the manifold perils of the Great War
were found faithful unto death

Neville F. W. Clarkson	Henry Pritchard
Alun E. Davies	William Roberts
John R. Davies	Matthew H. Stead
G. Tilston Haley	Evan P. Thomas
Arthur J. L. Hughes	W. Eric Thomas
J. Ivor Jones	Emyr J. Williams
R. Vernon Jones	Owen Williams
	(Benllech)
J. Francis Lewis	J. Newton Williams
Angus Mackay	W. Hugh Williams
Edward Owen	Matthew Williams
W. Jenkins Owen	Percy Williams

Do thou, for whom they died,
Live to serve as they served,
Valiant in action, steadfast in adversity,
Gentle in all things.

115

15

Nicknames are essential as a means of identification in Wales. How else could the Jones, Williams, Hughes, Owens, Griffiths, Evans and others be recognised in conversation.

They are acquired in a haphazard way. Thus Harry Pentir, (a place), Stanley the Post, and Lord Newborough - the latter, coming from a town of that name on the other side of the Island, was a bit of an outsider and thought to have too high an opinion of himself. 'The man with a hat' always wore a bowler tilted on the back of his head. He worked in a grocer's shop and on Sunday afternoons used to walk past our house with his bosom friend. The most taciturn of companions, they would stroll along on opposite sides of the road, minutely examining gutters and hedges and hardly saying a word.

One usually accepted such nicknames without much thought so although Jack General figures in my earliest recollections it was only recently I discovered how he got the name.

Jack was about six years older than I, shortish, strongly built with a nut brown face and dark curly hair. He was universally regarded as a bad lad and full of devilment. I never enquired into his origins but he had been adopted by a good but shrewish woman and her quiet, long-suffering husband.

By all accounts Jack devoted most of his energies when at school in Beaumaris to making life difficult for his teachers, while in the holidays he would often wander about on his own looking for mischief. His exit from his home in one of the cottages near Llanfaes Church was sometimes hurried. He was once seen racing through the open door and clearing the gate like a hurdler, followed by a torrent of abuse from his mother in hot pursuit with a sweeping brush.

One Summer's day when I was 4 he turned up at our house and asked politely if he could take Winnie and me out to play. Probably glad of a break, Mother agreed. So taking us by the hand Jack led us on to the road, chatting away merrily.

We made our first stop at the gate leading to Tre Castell farm and the beach. Swinging on gates was always tempting and the fact that it was forbidden gave it that extra spice.

This was a very wide iron gate with a marvellous squeak as it swung open. The bottom bar was brought to a halt by a large stone embedded in the ground while the top carried on for several inches to spring back in the most exciting way.

Jack said he would give us a swing. He began with gentle pushes that would have satisfied the most caring of mothers. But gradually he increased the speed until my pleasure turned to alarm and I asked to be put off.

"Just one more," said Jack and gave the gate one almighty shove. It swung round its 90 degrees in a second with the base jolting to an abrupt stop. The top whipped forward and in the shock of the recoil my grip was broken and I landed on my back.

Jack picked me up with apparent concern. But when I could see him again through the tears he was grinning like a Cheshire cat. Winnie, who had managed to hang on was shaken and said:

"Let's go home now, please."

"Not yet," said Jack, "We'll do some skipping."

He seized Winnie's skipping rope and began to skip along the road past the cottages. We followed like rats after the Pied Piper and were soon half way down the hill towards the beach. Here at the recessed entrance to the gravelled drive to Bryn Hyfryd with the large ornamental iron gate, Jack stopped and stood smiling at us while we smiled back.

"I know a good game. You're my prisoners-of-war and I've got to tie you up so you won't escape."

I didn't understand fully what he meant but it sounded good fun. He tied us both tightly round the waists and after making sure the knots were secure, he said:

I've got to go now, so I'll have to leave you. Goodbye."

I had no idea where we were. Home seemed miles away. As Jack disappeared I began to cry and Winnie soon joined in. After what seemed hours, Jack's grinning face appeared round the corner. He let us go on yelling for a while, taking in the scene. Then he came and untied us.

We begged to go home so Jack wrapped the skipping rope round the handles, gave it to Winnie and led us by the hands to our own gate, as cheerful as a cricket. He didn't take us in though but beat it as fast as he could.

He had the cheek to come a few days later to ask if he could take us out again. Mother said 'No', so he stopped calling and I had nothing to do with him for some years, though he used to attend the Evening Service intermittently.

The fun he'd been having at our expense, however, does

provide a clue to his nickname. It seems that in school when the boys played at soldiers, Jack always wanted to be the general.

When I was about 13 I got to talking to him on Sunday evenings after the service and as it was Summer time began to walk part of the way home with him across the fields.

Mother found out and remembering his past reputation I suppose, said he was too old for me. I should find someone of my own age, she said, although in fact there was none available at that time. I can understand her concern. But there was no need for it in spite of Jack's reputation. Like so many school tear-aways he had sobered into a steady, level-headed, law-abiding young man.

On leaving school he had been apprenticed to a blacksmith and once showed me to my amazement how much thicker his left wrist was than his right after five years working at the anvil. I'd always thought it would be the the other way round, the right being the striking arm. But as Jack explained, the left hand holding the tongs that held the horse-shoe had the biggest strain on it. Which reminded me of the white pony and how the smith used his left hand to pick up the cannon ball.

Jack was unrepentant about his school record and told me with some pride how Mr Roberts the headmaster had said when he was leaving, "Jack Hughes, you are the most badly behaved boy I have ever had in my school." And if the incident he related was true, I am not surprised.

He was once kept in school to be caned for misbehaviour. Instead of submitting he decided to run back into his class room to collect all the slates in a pile and sit waiting in a corner of the room opposite the door. The Head soon arrived with his cane and reinforced by his deputy. As soon as he opened the door Jack let fly with a slate that shattered on the wall.

"Good heavens," gasped the Head, "the boy's gone mad."

The two retreated to confer what to do next. Suspecting the police might be called, Jack took the opportunity of getting away through the window. Next morning he walked into school as bold as brass and took his punishment.

In spite of his nickname I think Jack was more of a loner than a leader. What his fate would have been in today's 'more enlightened' system with its army of social workers and psychiatrists is anyone's guess. As it was, like many adventurous young men of his time he was able to emigrate to Canada with his character intact. I never saw him again.

16

Most of us were snobs. That the gentry and better off were goes without saying. The poor were too. The had Holy Writ on their side. The rich man having to pass through the eye of a needle was a comforting thought.

Each group could find a way to feel superior to others. Church and Chapel, workers and n'er do wells, drinkers and teetotallers, Grammar and Council School pupils had their special claims to moral or material superiority.

How deplorable it was. What a nicely balanced stability it produced. Each little coterie grumbling away at the frailties of others and basking in the light of their own virtues.

In some ways it was more of a caste than a class system. To break out of ones caste was not easy. Money was the key but that provoked envy and the problem of acceptance by the higher caste.

There was a successful builder who had attended Penmon School years before. He had made his pile on Merseyside and returned to live in a fine house he had built. But he was not 'a gentleman' and perhaps wanting to retain some portion of his roots decided to send his two girls, aged about 10 and 8, to his old school.

They arrived unexpectedly one morning looking a little forlorn and standing out among the rest of us like lilies in a plot of buttercups and daisies. Looking much better dressed than the other girls they sat together in class. At play-time they stood apart from the rest, neither side able to bridge the gulf.

For the older boys they were as honey to wasps, with stares and smirks and sly comments. The day ended with their being seen off the premises with coarse remarks out of character with the usual friendly banter between the sexes. I was about 9 at the time and felt sorry for the girls who looked and probably were frightened. To the relief of the Head, I imagine, they never returned.

Father had little of the snob about him. He seemed at ease with everyone and was a good listener. As he grew older he would surprise me by asking complete strangers the most intimate questions without causing any apparent embarrassment.

Not so Mother. For her snobbery, (although she would not have accepted the word), was one of the keys to stability in the world. She had a minute knowledge of the interrelationships, the marriages, the social activities and moral lapses of the nobility and the gentry, keeping herself up to date with the gossip and Society Columns of the Daily papers and periodicals Father used to bring home by courtesy of Miss Pritchard.

At church she sang with conviction:

"The rich man in his castle, the poor man at his gate, God made them high or lowly and ordered their estate."

She once explained the tidy simplicity of it all.

"We don't expect to be invited into the houses of the gentry. At the same time there are people we wouldn't invite into ours."

She named a family which I will call the Jones'.

"Their ways are different to ours," she said. "They don't think as we do."

She regarded the Jones' as feckless. The husband was never in regular work while his wife, a cheerful, healthy little woman gave birth to a child every year. How they managed to survive in their small cottage was a mystery.

While believing there was no substitute for being 'to the manner born', Mother still thought it was up to everyone to better themselves - honestly, of course. For the likes of us education was important. So she was ready to 'make sacrifices' to send us to the Grammar School. By hard work one could step up the ladder.

When Tillis was commissioned in 1915 he had taken a step up and she was immensely proud of him. But how did that fit in with her rigid class system? Miss Pritchard at the time apparently had no doubts. Years before her brother had been a Regular Army Officer and was still known by his rank of Captain. What was the world coming to? The son of her gardener being allowed into the officer class. His commission was War-time, of course, and not the same. But - - .

Although she naturally said nothing to Mother outright, there was a perceptable coolness. Father, who knew the old lady better was not bothered. But Mother was hurt. And, illogical as it was, remembered the slight up to the time of Tillis' last illness.

The country parson, traditionally drawn from what was loosely called the 'gentleman' class, has enjoyed much latitude in conducting the affairs of his parish. Yet, as readers of Trollope will know, his status has varied enormously.

Our vicars, of whom there were three in my parents' time were all 'safe' men, unlikely to kick over the dogmatic or social traces. Of the first two I write only at second hand. Mr Kyffin, who used to visit Mother when she was first married, came to Llanfaes in 1889. His relationship with his working class parishioners seems to have been a happy one and as a product of Cheltenham and Oxford, he would doubtless have been on easy terms with the gentry.

My parents often spoke of him and also treasured a tangible memento of his encumbancy. In 1897 he invited all his parishioners to a party at the Vicarage to celebrate Queen Victoria's Diamond Jubilee and arranged for a photographer to record the event. The man was evidently a perfectionist and it took some time before he was satisfied the group was properly assembled on the lawn for the panoramic view he was about to take.

The result included Mother standing with one year old Ernie in her arms while Father is teetering on the right of the photo, in Mother's words, 'like a cat on hot bricks'. It was late afternoon and he was torn between pleasure and duty - whether to stay and appear on the photo for posterity to see or hurry away to close the lights on the greenhouses. Decisions such as this played havoc with Father's digestion.

In 1900 Mr Kyffin was followed by J D Jones, a clever young man with literary aspirations. A shop-keeper's son, he had made his way to Oxford and was to become editor of 'Handbooks for Sunday Schools' and joint translater of St Mark's Gospel into Welsh. He evidently took a keen interest in education for it was he who persuaded my parents to send Tillis to the Grammar School.

The Vicar in my time was from a different mould. Sturdily built and rubicund of countenance as befitted the son of a farmer, Mr Evans had graduated at Lampeter College in Mid-Wales. The most vivid impression I have of him is in his middle thirties, playing at half-back for Penmon when the team was starting up.

He was said to have been good in his day and was still worth his place in this embryo team. His face scarlet and glistening with sweat, determined yet half apologetic, he tries to tackle a fast young winger. Occasionally he succeeds and passes at once to a team mate. More often he is beaten and pulls up facing a non-existent opponent. He recovers and doggedly trails his man, now yards away racing for the corner flag to centre the ball.

His Pickwickian appearance was deceptive for behind it lay a shyness that fitted ill with his calling. While his smile was beaming, his conversation tended to be trivial and brief. We were his nearest neighbours and regular church-goers yet he rarely came to the house. When Father was dying he called to ask after him but excused himself when invited to come in to have a word with the old man.

He looked happiest in his Wellingtons, rounding up his cattle. Father, who defended him against all criticism, once went so far as to admit that Mr Evans would have made a better farmer than a parson. I think this is borne out by conversations I have had in recent years with old farming people. They remember with pleasure how he used to come round regularly and talk farming matters.

His services were correctly devout and his sermons monotonously dull. Where his parishioners were concerned his duties rarely seemed to extend beyond taking Sunday morning service. For the first few years he had officiated at Sunday School. But more and more he was content to leave its running to Father.

Until 1924 he lived the life of a bachelor cared for by a housekeeper. With the help of a handyman he kept his place spick and span, looked after his farm, tended his gardens and won prizes at the local show for his flowers and vegetables.

Winnie and I used to play on the wide earth bank between the field and the trees. We spent many happy hours on a swing tied to the branches of an oak that stretched a branch conveniently across. But because of a thick-set quickthorn hedge further along the bank we were unable to approach the Vicarage. Yet being so tantalisingly close it exercised a fascination over me. Surrounded by $5\frac{1}{2}$ acres of fields with outbuildings, an orchard and a lawn, it was like all the houses of the better off designed for privacy; hidden from the road by that narrow belt of trees and bushes, the dog-legged gravelled drive ran for more than 100 yards from the tall iron gate set back in a sector of high wall.

After a while I discovered that by jumping down into the woods I could work my way to see across the drive to the hedge on the other side and watch unseen anyone who passed along. Except for tradesmen there was little traffic and I was in no danger of being spotted. Telling no one of my adventure for fear of a ban, I soon became an Indian scout creeping through the undergrowth towards the Vicarage. Once I climbed on to the branch of a tree from which I could see parts of the house and faintly hear voices in conversation.

Sometimes I had the companionship of a red squirrel that would come quite near out of curiousity if I kept very still and pretended not to see it. In the Spring there were nests to look for. Mostly they would be blackbirds and thrushes. But once I found the nest of a long tailed tit with its enormous tail going in and out of the tiny hole in its large beautifully built home. I had a collection of wild birds' eggs but knew that although there would be at least a dozen inside I dare not even touch it for fear the parents would abandon them.

The fascination of the woods declined as my interests widened. So when I was 12 the change that came to the Vicarage was of no great concern to me in spite of the gossip it produced. The Vicar was about to marry. The lady of his choice was the daughter of a retired draper, widow of an engineer and mother of two boys and a girl.

There was speculation that with a wife to support him the Vicar would start up again some of the pastoral activities the parishioners has enjoyed under his predecessors. Most were sceptical. Mother stressed the obvious that leopards did not change their spots and pointed out that though uninspiring, the Vicar was solid and reliable. It might be no bad thing if things remained as they were.

Early in 1925 the marriage took place very quietly and the sceptics were soon proved right. If anything we saw less of the Vicar and of his wife, nothing at all. Of the reasons for this there was naturally much gossip. Personally I never once saw the lady so presume she must have become a recluse for reasons of her own.

During the Easter holidays something happened that may provide a clue. One of our nearest neighbours had a nephew who used to come from his home in Manchester to stay with them for a holiday. He and I used to play togetner and on this occasion happened to be messing about outside the entrance to the Vicarage. Quite suddenly the gate opened and a boy appeared. He spoke to my companion who was nearest to him.

My mother has sent me to ask you if you would like to come and play with me."

My friend replied with alacrity that he would and moved

towards the gate. For what came next the ambiguity of English Grammar must bear some of the responsibility. After all, the boy did say 'you', which could be either singular or plural. I was about to follow when he said:

"No, not you. Mother didn't say you."

I was a snub that most of us have to swallow at some time. But what rankled with me was the way my 'friend' had accepted the invitation and walked away without a word or a glance. I couldn't understand why he had been singled out either.

I asked Mother. Knowing her way though the maze of class-distinction she said she was not surprised. She smiled and added:

"Don't you see? Gerald goes to Manchester Grammar School and that makes all the difference."

So that was it. I knew Public Schools were superior. Now it seemed not all Grammar Schools were equal. Manchester was superior to Beaumaris: higher up the social ladder. I was not invited because I attended an inferior school.

Not so long after I realised there could be a flaw in this reasoning. The Vicar's step-daughter, Mary, came to the Beaumaris one. She used to cycle there with Winnie and me. A few years ago Mary reminded me of something I'd forgotten. We used to compete to see who could learn most verses from the Bible for Sunday School.

Many houses had warning notices prominently displayed:
NO HAWKERS, BEWARE OF THE DOG, and TRESPASSERS WILL BE PROSECUTED.

The word 'trespass' had me confused when I was small. I thought it had to do with property. And as I did not go on other people's I tended to feel self-righteous when praying for my trespasses to be forgiven.

The front door of all the larger houses was strictly reserved for visitors of the genteel sort. Servants, tradesmen and ordinary folk went round to the back. Even the hoi polloi if they were able, made a distinction between front and back as a sign of respectability. Our front door was kept locked, partly as a safety precaution, but when Miss Pritchard had sent to inform Mother that she would be calling, (as she did quite regularly in her last years), the key was turned ready.

I was rarely obliged to call at any of the larger houses but when I did I walked round to the back as a matter of course. The one exception had unpleasant conseequences.

It was a house occupied by someone with some pretentions

to gentility, employing a chauffeur-handyman who lived with his family on the premises. As we had made friends with his children, Winnie and I decided one day to go and visit them. The only entrance to the house was a short drive so we went up intending to walk round to the back. As we got near, a 'lady' suddenly appeared and advanced upon us shouting:

"Where do you think you are going? Get off my property at once you dirty brats," and some other comments of the same nature.

I was 10 at the time and Winnie 12, so we were of an age not to be completely overawed, but we had to retreat bewildered and angry.

Mother and Father were furious; not so much at our being ordered off as at the epithets hurled at us. The word 'dirty' particularly caught Mother on the raw. Their friend the chauffeur was even more so at the interference with his private life. He handed in his notice after telling his employer exactly what he thought of her; and being a man of good character soon obtained other employment.

At the time Mother outlined her belief in the rigid social order the War was just over and we had not yet felt the impact of the great changes set in train by that world-shatterand event. So for a while it had seemed logical enough. But there came a time when logic had little to do with human relationships.

I must have been about 14 when Mother shook me out of a deep sleep at 2 o'clock one morning. The eldest Jones' boy had just come in an agitated state to knock us up and say the baby his mother was expecting was about to arrive prematurely. Would I cycle to Beaumaris for the doctor. Mother added that meanwhile she was going to see what she could do to help.

It was a moonlight night in late Spring and the ride at that unusual hour was exhilarating. I knocked up the doctor who set off in his car while I rode home. All went well and yet another baby was delivered to the Jones family.

By 1933 the elder children were working and helping to support the family that had continued to grow until just over a year before. Since then Mrs Jones' health had gradually deteriorated and she had not been seen out for several weeks. Then, in the late Autumn it was known that she was in the terminal stage of cancer.

Mother had for some time been going every evening to sit with her, taking cooked delicacies and giving what help and comfort she could. For my part I had hardly exchanged more than the days greetings with the little woman since I had known her. But now she expressed a wish to see me, remembering, so Mother said, how I had gone to fetch the doctor and also because I was leaving next day to join the Army.

Early that dull November evening I entered the sick room to find it so dimly lit by a small lamp near the bed in the corner that at first I could hardly make out objects at all clearly. Mother beckoned me over and said:

"Here's Arthur come to say goodbye. You know he's going away tomorrow.'

I went over and looked down at the bed. With profound shock I saw that the sturdy little woman I had known was shrunk to the size of a wizened child. Ill at ease and at a loss what to say I was glad that Mother did most of the talking over the next ten minutes.

At last she said, "You'd better say goodbye now. Mrs Jones mustn't get too tired."

Uncertain what to do I leant over the bed to take her hand. But the dying woman reached up and clung to me with sudden intensity. Conscious of her agony and fear I felt at once embarrassed and helpless. For she must have known that death was near.

I left for Aldershot the next day and soon cast off thought of that disturbing experience in the excitement of a new life. Yet more than half a century later I can feel again the despair of that desperate embrace and my own inadequacy.

17

The school roll varied between 50 and 60. Of these about 20 were in the top classes. I think the Head's methods were about right for the time. We all had to work but no one was pushed too hard. Nearly all left school able to read well and do sums. Most expected to find work on farms, in the local quarries, in service or for some small business employer.

A few of the brightest were given special tuition for entry to the Grammar school at Beaumaris. Scholarships were few but if a child could reach the modest entrance standards, many parents were ready to make sacrifices to pay for their children to have the chance to 'better themselves'.

The exam was fair enough in that we were told exactly what to expect. Mechanical arithmetic for speed and, (this was before IQ came in fashion), problems for testing the intelligence. We had to analyse sentences into Subject, predicate and Object with their various qualifications and modifications. This basic training has stood me in good stead over the years.

Then there was the essay in which spelling, grammar and paragraphing counted as much as the modicum of originality possessed by the average 11 or 12 year old.

Mr Thomas prepared the half dozen who were going to sit. Towards the end he gave us Scholarship Tests from the Teachers' World. But apart from the formal stuff the part I remember was the rare occasions he read extracts to us from the literary classics. He would ping the little bell at the front of his desk. Our hands would fly to our heads and he would call us out to stand round his desk.

It was there I had my first introduction to Shakespeare in Mark Antony's oration from 'Julius Caesar' and Henry V's Speech before Agincourt . He must have read them well for although he gave only brief introductions I can still recall the feeling of tension as Antony developed his ironic references to the conspirators as 'noble men' and Henry V's:

"No my fair cousin,
If we are marked to die we are enow
To do our country loss, and if to live,
The fewer men the greater share of honour."

One other piece I remember well - the Schoolmaster from Goldsmith's 'Deserted Village'.

"A man severe he was and stern to view;
I knew him well, and every truant knew."

As he read we, or at least I was comparing the famous pedagogue with our own Mr T. And I'm sure the thought was on his mind too

At odd times Mr Thomas would leave the classroom and take a turn round the yard, sometimes presaging his exit by a reprimand to some child for some trifling mistake. Wynn once told me his father had had sun-stroke when he was young and still had headaches that could only be relieved by going out into the fresh air.

This sounded perfectly reasonable and in any case we were only too pleased to be left unattended. Not that we dared to get up to much mischief. If a boy moved out of his place or engaged in some foolery, he would soon made aware of his mistake by the exaggerated attention the rest were paying to their work. Looking up he would see Mr T's head at the window. The shock and a word of caution on Mr T's return to the room were enough to make him more careful from then on,

Had we been more worldly wise we might have deduced another reason than the effects of sunstroke for out Head's taking to the fresh air. This was a habit he had of slipping a peppermint into his mouth from time to time. He was inordinately partial to peppermints.

My chances of gaining a scholarship were not highly rated. Although my English was good, my arithmetic was erratic. Fortunately there was not the pressure on us from school or parents that in later years became associated with the 11+. I wanted to do well but did not feel over anxious.

On the morning of the exam, Mother saw me to the gate and told me to do my best. I did not take much notice of this as my overriding concern was to get there in time - an attitude of mind which affected most of my generation and is still hard to throw off. The walk to Beaumaris was no trouble. I was worried about whether I could find the place in the Grammar School where the exam was held.

Of course it turned out quite easy. A trickle of boys and girls pointed the way. And when I reached the school yard some were standing in groups, most looking as overawed as I felt. Only the odd extrovert looked at ease, cracking school-

128

boy jokes and egged on by the self-conscious giggles of his audience.

In the exam room we were seated in individual desks, which was a novel experience as most of us were used to the bench type that seated four. We were marshalled by a thin, stern-faced, sharp-tongued mistress who appeared to have a particular dislike of boys and whom I later came to know as a severe but dedicated teacher of English.

When the first exam papers were given out I was relieved to find there was nothing I had not been taught. But the only question I can now remember was in the Essay paper:

'Give an account of your favourite character in fiction.'

I chose Oliver Twist, having only recently heard Father read the whole book and talk about it in the normal course of conversation as he so often did with Dickens.

Results oc the exam used to come through quickly in those days. To the family's delight I had come fourth and was the only one from our school to win a scholarship.

That evening Mr Thomas called at the house on his way home from Beaumaris. He was wheeling his bike as he invariably did on his way home. He seemed very pleased with me. I felt a little embarrassed though as even to my inexperienced eye he was a bit tipsy. When he had gone Father laughed and commented that he was "three sheets in the wind all right".

That weekend I was fancying myself quite a bit at my unexpected success. But on Monday I learnt the hard lesson of how soon success can turn to ashes. No one mentioned the word 'scholarship', nor was it spoken for the rest of the term. Mr Thomas wished all those who were leaving success and mentioned that three boys were going to the Grammar School as they had passed the entrance exam.

In retrospect I realise how fortunate I had been. For the school system was completely English orientated. All teaching in the Grammar School, except for the few who took Welsh as a 'foreign' language was in English. From the outset, with my home background I had been given a flying start.

18

On 25th August 1925 the news broke that Miss Pritchard was dead. She was 80 and although we knew she had been failing, it still came as a shock. Father had been with her for forty years and so far as I know they had had only one difference. This was soon after I was born when, with five children to support, he asked her for a rise in pay from £2 to £2 10s a week. She gave it grudgingly, adding that he could expect nothing in her will.

Over the next few years she must have had a change of heart, for in 1920 she made a will in which she left him £500. Another sign of favour came in 1924 when she paid him to go to the British Empire Exhibition at Wembley. It was Father's only visit to London and he returned with a Wembley Broach and full of the wonders of the Exhibition and the people he had met.

The will stood, so with £500 and some savings he was assured of 10/ a week at 4%. That, with the 'Lloyd George', my parents felt, made their old age secure.

The only other servant to receive a substantial sum was David Jones the butler who got £750. This seems to have been due to a sentimental attachment to her retainer by Miss Pritchard, for the old fellow seems to have been steadily depleting her wine cellar.

Kyffin Williams says that when, as a small boy, he visited her, the butler was obviously 'under the influence' and kept spilling the tea. Miss Pritchard expostulated with:

"David: you're drunk."

To which he replied:

"Not drunk, Miss. Just a bit drunky wunky."

One can only surmise that the Old Lady, knowing he would have little chance of re-employment, was doing her best to provide for his future.

I now see her death as symbolic of the end of an era; the time when the dismemberment of large estates, hastened by high taxation and death duties made it impossible to employ large numbers of people in a multiplicity of domestic roles.

The Bryn Hyfryd farm went to one niece; the house and grounds to another - Essylt Williams, who was married to a Bank Manager. Before they took possession early in 1926 with their two young sons, we moved in as caretakers.

Father continued to tend the gardens while I helped in the holidays and weekends for pocket money. Dick and John the two boys used to follow Father around and were keenly interested in what he was doing. The story of how the Williams' were forced to leave is graphically told by Kyffin (John) in his autobiography ACROSS THE STRAITS. Another niece that Miss Pritchard had cut out of her will, brought a court case for some of the furniture. She lost, but so crippled the Williams' with court costs, they had to sell up and depart.

The place was bought by Geoffrey Williams, a cousin of the family. Of him Kyffin writes that 'he seemed to be mentally unbalanced', and from my observation this was not an over-statement.

But the important thing for us was that Father retained his job and when Geoffrey left after a brief stay he was kept on as a sort of caretaker and allowed to use part of the garden and the cool greenhouse to grow produce for sale at the greengrocer's in Beaumaris. In this way he was eased into retirement when over 70.

For myself I will mention three instances when I found it difficult to pull myself together.

In 1932 I qualified as a teacher with the recession in full flood. Ten thousand of us had been taken on in expectation of the school leaving age being raised. It did not materialise and after months of unemployment and temporary work I enlisted as a clerk in the RASC in November 1933. I had often felt that Mother would have liked me to be her confidant as Tillis had been. I knew I could never step into his shoes. But out of gratitude, or perhaps conscience, I made out a third of my Army pay, (5/- out of 15/3d a week), to her and Father as recompense for having supported my education over all those years and to make their lives a little easier.

In 1937 I was posted abroad. Father was 75 and as I said goodbye it crossed my mind that I might never see him again. Mother was 64 and seemed happy and in good health. The War came and in 1941 she wrote me a long letter telling me about their Golden Wedding, how well things had turned out for them and how contented they were with their lot.

My posting stretched out from three to over five years, but after several applications, orders to return home came in Jan-

uary 1943. The day before I was due to sail a cablegram arrived informing me that Mother had died. Death was so com-
monplace I did not look for sympathy. I went to the only
private place, the loo, to pull myself together by having a
good cry.

In October 1944, when in Oswestry I met Barbara, a Liverpool girl who was a RADAR Technical Instructor. We were
married within a month. After 38 years of sharing joys and
sorrows she died in her sleep nearly four years ago. She was
61. I have a grown-up son and daughter; but the difficulties
of pulling myself together only those who have suffered such
a loss will understand. I think my childhood experiences of
being alone without being lonely was a help.

For the rest, we could hardly be called a closely knit family. Without Edith I doubt whether I would know anything
about the rest.

Ernie became a successful agent with the Liver Friendly
Society, ending up with two books after the War. We fell out
over something I wrote in a letter for which he demanded an
apology. I refused and after Father's funeral I saw him only
once. He was executor for the will and turned up one afternoon at the door of a classroom at Brae Street School where
I was teaching. All he said was:

"Here's the cheque for your share of the will."

I thanked him. We looked at each other a moment, then he
turned and walked away.

I closed the door and saw that one thirteen year old boy
was smiling.

"I know him," he said. "He comes to ar' 'ouse for the in-
surance. 'e takes it out of yer 'air."

Ernie retired with a dicky heart when he was 55 to Old
Colwyn where he lived in financial comfort to the age of 69.
He died in his chair watching Television.

After seven years in the Army, Jack spent two with the
Palestine Police. He returned in 1931 to several years of odd
jobs and unemployment. I was best man at his wedding in
Dorking in June 1937, just before the Coronation of George
VI. The day before the ceremony we went to London where I
wanted to buy a Morgan Three-wheeler. We were going down
a street with Jack at the wheel when I happened to look
back and saw we were followed by clouds of black smoke. As
we drove back feeling we had been conned, Jack remarked:

"Do you think a punch on the nose might help?"

That not being my way of doing things, I said no, thinking to myself, 'same old Jack'.

The engine was quickly replaced, the firm regarding the hole in the crank-case as just a bit of bad luck.

After the wedding the bride and groom drove ahead in a hired car, making for Wales, while I followed in the Morgan, Soon after we started the gear lever snapped off leaving me stranded at a traffic light. A phone call to the dealer and a car soon turned up with a replacement.

At this point Jack and Ivy decided enough was enough and drove off. My misfortunes continued when the car stalled and I got out to crank up only to find I'd left the starting handle in and it must have fallen out somewhere miles back. I pushed the car to a nearby garage where a sympathetic mechanic spent half an hour adapting the handle of another car charging me 5/-. Driving all night I arrived at Copthorne Barracks in Shrewsbury, where I was Education Instructor, at 5am and promptly went to bed.

I never saw Jack after Father's funeral. We did not fall out - just drifted apart with him in the South and me on Merseyside. I heard from Edith he was dead. He was 71 and collapsed in the street to die instantly. When the news sank in I broke down. Somehow I felt that the cards had fallen badly for Jack and that he never had the chance to play the ones he was dealt.

Only Winnie died in hospital. We saw her at Edith's where she was staying. She was not well and as usual had little to say. When cancer was diagnosed she carried herself bravely and Edith cared for her until near the end.

Barbara and I used to visit Edith every summer after she was widowed in 1955. When her only son married she lived contentedly alone in rural Lincolnshire, entering into the life of the little community. At 81 her death came peacefully. She was sitting up in bed reading the Sunday newspaper when her heart stopped.

About the age of 15 I lost my faith and ever since have been an agnostic, happy to say 'I don't know' and leave it at that. I have never found this an obstacle in my relations with others. One of the best friends I ever had was a vicar I first met nearly fifty years ago. When I told him I was an agnostic he replied: "No matter. Some of my best friends are." A trusted friend comes of an Irish Catholic family.

I have long been a student of history, which may be a sort of substitute for religion: connecting the present with the past; trying to understand how our forebears felt and thought and what motivated them. And as it is impossible to have a proper understanding of Western Civilization without a sound knowledge of the King James' Bible and of Christianity, I can count myself fortunate to have imbibed them when a child.

My earliest recollection was on the mystery of Time; and in my later years this has, perhaps naturally, recurred. At times I am spurred on by the lines from Andrew Marvell's beautiful love poem:

But at my back I always hear
Time's winged chariot hurrying near.

And I think back to Sunday evenings in the old Church Room to hear again the harmonium with the stops out and the full throated singing of the congregation - - 'Time like an ever rolling stream, bears all its sons away; they fly forgotten as a dream dies at the opening day'.

Like a dream, maybe. Yet in my mind those I have written about and others I have known, are as alive as the friend I was with only a few days ago. And as long as I can keep on pulling myself together, so it will remain. And after that, well, in the words of the song, I guess it doesn't matter any more.

END.

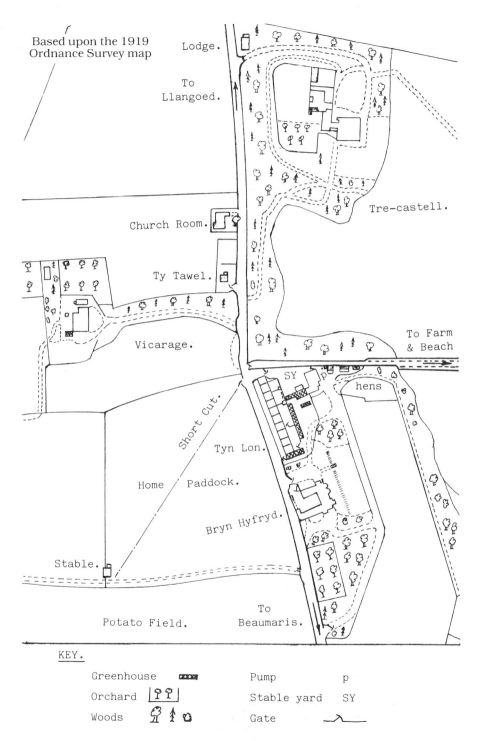

Based upon the 1919
Ordnance Survey map

Lodge.

To
Llangoed.

Church Room.

Ty Tawel.

Tre-castell.

Vicarage.

To Farm
& Beach

SY

hens

Short Cut.

Tyn Lon.

Home / Paddock.

Bryn Hyfryd.

Stable.

To
Beaumaris.

Potato Field.

KEY.

Greenhouse	Pump	p
Orchard	Stable yard	SY
Woods	Gate	

135

SCALE.

```
0        1        2
|---|---|---|        kilometers
                     miles
0                1
```

KEY.

Roads	
Railway	
Beach	
Hospital	H
Lighthouse	

Puffin
Island

Quarry

Penmon

Llanddona

Llangoed

Tre-castell

Bryn Hyfryd

Lifeboat Station

Llanfaes

Fryars

Baron
Hill

Castle

BEAUMARIS

Red Hill

Llandegfan

Garth

Ferry

MENAI
BRIDGE

BANGOR

Based upon the 1971 Ordnance Survey 1/50,000, map with the permission
of the controller of Her Majesty's Stationery Office,
Crown Copyright Reserved.